A Pensioner's Folly

Sailing 15,400 miles in a small boat from the UK to New Zealand

Chris Ayres

Chris Ayres is a sailor, climber and adventurer. For many years he was was a climbing and outdoor pursuits instructor and qualified "Guide de Haute Montagne", taking clients climbing, mountaineering and treking. This took him to many mountain ranges in different parts of the world. He confesses to always having a bit of travel bug. He hitch hiked to India many years ago.

He came late to sailing, starting off on a friend's boat but soon bought a small yacht and learnt how to be a sailor. He cruised the Irish sea around Anglesey, North Wales and from South Wales up to the Isle of Man, Lake District, Scotland and across to Ireland. One summer he circumnavigated Ireland.

Later he sold his first boat and bought "Sea Bear" a Vancouver 28.

The blog and pictures of Sea Bear can be found at :
www.seabear.uk

Cover picture Morea from Maeve Bay, Tahiti

Copyright © 20211 Chris Ayres
All rights reserved
ISBN-13

Acknowledgments

I would like to thank all those unnamed and unmentioned people in all the countries I visited.

All the people who served me in shops, in bars, in restaurants, in markets and from street stalls and the customs officers and officials, all those workers in boat yards, all those passers-by who gave me a wave or a smile or stopped for a chat. Thank you all for making me feel welcome in your countries and making my time there so enjoyable.

Contents

1. A scare and beginnings	2
2. Across Biscay	6
3. Coasting in Spain	9
4. Into Portuguese waters	18
5. Spain Again	33
6. To Morocco	36
7. Off to the Canaries	41
8. Bound for the Cape Verde Islands	52
9. Atlantic Crossing	57
10. Cruising through the Leeward Isles	67
11. Heading South to Trinidad	87
12. Up through the Windwards and Leewards	104
13. To the British Virgin Islands and Dominican Republic	118
14. Hiati and Cuba.	127
15. Sister Islands Caves and Dragons and Jamaica	136
16. How I set off for Curacao and ended up in Panama	143
17. Panama, Guna Yala and the canal	150
18. Las Perlas and passage to Galapagos	165
19. Passage to Marquesas	172
20. Tahiti	186
21. The Iles Sous le Vent	191
22. Passage to Tonga	196
23. Kingdom of Tonga	202
24. Passage to New Zealand	209
The Boat	213
Glossary	216

1. A scare and beginnings

"Preparation is the most important part of cruising." (Lin and Larry Pardey)

The squall when it hit was vicious. I had no warning of it coming, it was drizzly and misty that morning with poor visibility. The wind which had been about 8-10 knots suddenly hit 35 - 40 knots and the rain was torrential. I was grateful that I hadn't shaken out my precautionary overnight reef in the main sail. Even so the boat was laid over on its ear, the lee gunwale awash. The situation was perilous, there was no time to don waterproofs. In the cockpit I struggled to furl the yankee and then carefully made my way to the foot of the mast to down the main sail. It was a hard struggle hauling down hand by hand the wet slippery sail which was full of wind, to leave me running under just the storm staysail. It hit me then, the reality of my situation. I was alone in the Southern Pacific ocean, 14 days out from the Galapagos Islands over 1,000 miles in my wake and bound for the Marquesas still 2,000 miles away. Far from any shipping lanes, I was far away from any help, I just had to manage on my own. Clad in just vest and shorts, the wind driven rain stung and by the time I had got the situation more or less under control I was drenched to the skin. But at least then I could retreat to the cabin to dry off and take stock.

How had I come to be here? I was sailing my boat, Sea Bear, singlehanded across the Pacific. 3 years before, a few months after retiring from work age 66, I had left the UK and I was following the classic trade winds routes perhaps with a circumnavigation in mind.

"She and her kind were never built so that men should stay quietly at home. She breathes sturdy eager confidence, a living embodiment of the truth that the sea is for sailing, that strenuousness is the immortal path and sloth the way of death." (W.H. Tilman)

First I should tell you a little about Sea Bear. She is a Vancouver, 28ft long and was built by Northshore in 1987. I bought her late in 2012 and in 2013 I sailed her single handed from the Solent to North Wales where I had a swinging mooring. Later that summer I sailed over to east coast of Ireland and took in the Isle of Man and the Lake District on return.

Towards Christmas of 2013, with retirement from work imminent, it gradually dawned on me that I had the boat that was capable of a big trip. Dreams of big sailing trips had lain long dormant in my mind since as a teenager I had been inspired by books of sailing adventures. I just never thought that things like that were in my reach, but here I was, I had the boat, the question was was I up to it?

Gradually plans took shape and I thought I must at least try. Being a mountaineer I had always thought that I might follow in Tilman's footsteps and head to cold mountainous islands, but some warmth appealed to me. The plan thus was to head south to the Canaries then the Cape Verde Islands and across to the Caribbean. I thought I might continue through the Panama canal to the Galapagos and so across the Pacific to eventually, New Zealand. Once there, well it has half way around so I might just carry on, a gentle leisurely circumnavigation. I pencilled in the beginning of August to depart.

The time following my retirement in June leading up to departure were hectic to say the least. A thousand questions to answer and decisions to take, what to do with the house, possessions, the car, the cat? Does the boat need anything doing? Charts and courtesy flags to buy. Then all the arrangements to make. At some points I doubted that I could get everything done in time.

A week before my pencilled in departure date I moved Sea Bear from her swinging mooring to a berth in Caernarfon dock. Alongside it would be much easierto do those last minute jobs, move my stuff aboard and provision for the trip.

I had just berthed in the dock when to my surprise two old friends turned up on the quayside all the way from Cumbria to wish me well. They and my sailing mentor and his partner took me out for a lovely curry and gave me a present of a fine single malt.

Jobs done, provisions and gear aboard we just needed a suitable weather slot. For days we had strong southerly winds F6 and 7, the legacy of hurricane Bertha, not the conditions for crossing Caernarfon Bar, but the forecast spoke of an improvement on the Monday so departure was planned for that afternoons tide.

I had not been my intention to go single handed. I had arranged crew to go with me and they turned up in Caernarfon apparently all ready to go. However with less than 24 hours to go they dropped out. It left me in an awkward spot. I didn't want to miss the weather window or leave any later, it was already mid August and I wanted to be across Biscay before September was out. Without crew, my insurance would not be valid but I was unlikely to find another crew member at such short notice. It didn't take me long however to decide to just go alone. It made me a little nervous as I had never undertaken such a long passage solo before but I wasn't about to let a little setback get in the way of months of effort and planning.

2. Across Biscay

"The interesting thing about an offshore trip on a small boat is that you untie more than the boat when you slip the mooring." (Pete Goss)

I set out as planned on the Monday afternoon. Conditions were still a bit bouncy over the bar and not much better outside. There had been strong southerly winds for a week and now it was north- west winds so the sea was a bit confused. Bardsey Island was rounded in the dark and a course set for the Smalls. A rough night and the skipper wasn't feeling at his best. Gradually the next day conditions improved, the winds fell lighter and Sea Bear could wear her full set of sails. Our first dolphins of this trip came to play around the boat in the late afternoon. The red lights on the Scillies radio tower were spotted during the second night, they were visible a long way out. Passing to the west of the Seven Stones rocks we were that close to the Scillies that it seemed a shame not to drop in, so I did, picking up a mooring in St Mary's pool. It was a good opportunity to catch up on sleep. The Scillies looked a fascinating place to cruise so I had a slight regret about not stopping longer, but there was no time this time, the south called.

I departed the Scillies on Friday morning under a gentle northwest breeze, too gentle really. I had the cruising chute up for the first time ever, but handed it just before dark. A 24 hr run of just 64 miles which took us into French waters, disappointingly slow progress really. Sometimes one needs the patience of a saint to be a sailor. More dolphins and yes out here the water really was blue. On the 2nd day I had changed the yankee for the big genoa but by the afternoon of the 3rd day I had a struggle to hand it on account of the rising wind and I rehoist the yankee. I got a bit of a scare when I heard the tail end of the shipping forecast with bad reception 'Sole gale F8 perhaps storm force 10.' Slightly relieved when I heard later that forecast was for NW Sole but bad enough was NW Biscay SW F5-7 and gale F8. I was glad that I was 50 miles or so to the Atlantic side of the continental shelf with plenty of sea room.

It was unpleasant enough as it was but I did see a whale which surfaced alongside. I was first aware of a spray of mist past the sprayhood as it blew and there it was about 15 feet off - amazing.

Monday late afternoon I was lured into thinking the worst was past, the forecast had predicted it to ease and for some hours the wind had been a manageable 20 to 25 knots and the sea state had eased and I had shaken out the third reef in the main. It saved the worst for a dark night and winds of 30 - 35 knots, a particularly low point was having to put the third reef back, in wind and driving rain.

However by Tuesday things were improving though I was still losing westing. All this time I had intended Coruna as my arrival point in Spain but Wednesday's southwest winds look like putting paid to that. In the end I made it to Ria Ribadeo and motored into the marina with the last light in the sky. A helpful marina hand waved me to a pontoon and helped with my lines. Formalities were soon completed, a much needed shower was taken. Sitting in the cockpit a beautiful 15 year old single malt, given as a departure gift from true friends, was broached as a celebration of a single handed Biscay crossing.

3. Coasting in Spain

"In venturing in sail upon strange coasts we are seeking those first experiences, and trying to feel as felt the earlier man in a happier time, to see the world as they saw it." (Hilaire Belloc)

Ria Ribadea is one of the Rias Atlas that are found on this northwestern corner of Spain, Galacia. They are sunken estuaries and have been compared to Scottish sea lochs. Maybe so, they are a bit more developed, with no midges and warmer. It was now September and I was sailing in shorts and t-shirt. I hadn't planned to visit them but I am very glad that I did. They are very beautiful and the coast is somewhat rugged. After a few days in Ribadea in which I enjoyed wandering the streets, I spent several nights at anchor in Ria de Viveiro and then in Ria Cedeira. I met an interesting French journalist, Jean Mitchell who used to work for Le Figero. He swam across from his anchored Wharram cat and invited me across for drinks. Like me he was headed south.

I did visit Coruna in the end. It was not really my sort of a place, big city and high prices, but I needed a decent chandlery for some charts and a vhf antenna. On the street map Casa Museo Picasso was marked, so I found my way there. By a wooden door between 2 shops was a small sign with opening hours, yes it was open but the door shut. A bell for the 2nd floor was simply marked Picasso so I rang it. After a brief pause the door clicked open and I entered a dark hallway, a dark wooden staircase lead upwards in almost complete darkness and on the 2nd floor a door was ajar. Entering, I was in the apartment that Picasso lived in in his time in Galicia. It had been either preserved or restored to how it must have been. It was long and thin, several rooms with simple furniture, a table with open notebooks under glass cases, a room that acted as a studio with an easel and paints and reproduction Picasso prints on the wall. A young Spaniard was the guardian but he had no english and my spanish is still so rudimentary. Nevertheless it was quite a remarkable experience.

Leaving Coruna under a grey sky a notable landmark was the Tower of Hercules. This was built by the Romans and is the oldest functioning lighthouse in the world. A sail of some 35 miles, some engine assisted as the winds were so light, led me past more rugged coastline and past the rocky Islas Sisarga and then having passed Punta del Roncudo I turned into the Ria de Corme Y Laxe. Here I anchored off the beach at Laxe for the night.

I woke in the night to thick fog but it had cleared by morning and it looked like a lovely day was in store. Sailing past more rugged coastline was the order of the day and with plenty of unmarked offshore rocks about, due diligence was paid to careful navigation. Rounding the spectacular headland of Cabo Villane I entered Ria de Camarinas. The fishing village of Camarinas is in another of the delightful Rias Atlas. It is more or less unspoilt and less developed than others. That evening I ate barbecued sardines at a bar. But you wouldn't get these sardines into a tin, they were about 8 inches long. They barbecue them on the roadside outside the bars and serve them on a plate with just some fresh bread, no knives or forks just eat them with your fingers, washed down with a beer. They were delicious.

A couple of days bad weather kept me in Camarinas, but then it was time to round Cabo Finisterre. There was no wind so it meant a deal of motoring but at least conditions were calm, with just a little swell, for rounding this notable cape. Further on down this "Costa del Morte" I decided to take the inshore passage inside the unmarked rocks of Bajos los Meixidos and los Bruyos. They do poke above the water though and the swell breaking over them gives a clear indication of their whereabouts. Passing Punta Queixal and its off-lying rocks we entered the Ria Muros and proceeded to Muros where we anchored off the town outside the harbour.

Leaving Muros it was a bright and sunny morning. However I'd not gone far when I ran into one of the area's renowned mists. The sun could still be glimpsed overhead but the visibility was not good. Several times I thought of turning back but soon I was outside the ria and so I carried on. Thank goodness for GPS and AIS. Experience had shown over the past days that almost all Spanish fishing boats were fitted with and used AIS so that was some reassurance but the trouble with fog at sea sometimes is you just cannot tell how far you can see, is it 50 or 200 meters? Needless to say a nervous watch was kept. Later the visibility did improve and then it eventually cleared altogether, another hot sunny day off the Spanish coast.

As if I hadn't enough excitement for one day I decided to take the Canal de Norte to enter Ria Arousa, it all looked straightforward enough with care and indeed it was all going well apart from a port hand red mark which was marked on the chart and pilot but was missing. The white and green tower starboard mark on Pedras del Sargo was clear enough though and I watched several fishing boats go through. Then the rock awash to the channel side of the tower was spotted. Dead slow, give the tower a wider berth, but how far since there were no other marks, watch that forward echo sounder closely, we were past. That was a nasty surprise.

Further up the ria, which really should be named Ria de Mejillon, from all the vivaros used for cultivating mussels, we anchored off Playa Arena de la Secada at the northern end of the Isla de Arousa. A very pleasant spot indeed. I should explain vivaros are big floating rafts from which they hang ropes on which the mussels (mejillon) grow.

It seemed the thing to do whilst in the area to pay a visit to Santiagio de Compostello. Accordingly next morning I put into the marina in Villagarcia de Arousa just a few miles further up the ria. The marker on the end of the breakwater is a huge mussel stood on end.

I then took the train to Santiagio de Compostello to play at being a proper tourist. I was impressed by the train, fast and cheap and with more leg room than on British trains. Santiagio de Compostello is of course famous for its cathedral and the old town with its narrow streets between stone buildings and is a site of pilgrimage. So as you would expect very touristy and full of tourists. I'm pleased I went but glad it was just for an afternoon. My last bit of time there was spent drinking beer next to an impromptu session with a Venezuelan and a Spaniard who were playing guitar and singing traditional songs - lovely. After the train back I ate outside a tapas bar along with crowds of chattering Spanish. By the end of the day my head was just full of noise.

I quite liked Villagarcia, an unpretentious working town. There were parks, a good beach from which I had my first swim in the sea for many years and the marina was cheap. I could have stayed on for much longer but it was time to move on to the next ria.

The day started with a gentle sail, beam reaching down the ria but turning southwest past the Illa de Arousa it was a beat. Past the Isla de Rua which just seems like a heap of gigantic granite boulders we had a mad half hour where I went from yankee, staysail and full main down to 2 reefs in main and just a furled yankee in 3 stages with 25 knots of wind oh yes and heavy rain too. It kicked up quite a sea too. Soon the wind was back to normal and I was back to a full set of sails but the sloppy sea and now light winds made sailing difficult. I rounded the Peninusla de O Grove and headed for the gap between the Illa de Ons and the mainland. Eventually it was just one tack too many and if I wanted to make the anchorage at Bueu before dark I accepted that I would have use the engine so I finished the passage by motoring past Picamillo tower and into the Ria Pontevedra. Crossing the ria and passing through lines of vivaros I arrived at Bueu where I anchored off the beach in time to watch the sunset.

In the end I stayed at anchor at Bueu for 3 nights. There were 3 other boats here, an interesting contrast in style. A big old wooden Norwegian Gaffer, a Halberg Rassy 50 all mod cons and power hungry, they were running the engine to power the washing machine, and a Wyloe , these seem the boat of choice by a number of liveaboards. Next day I inflated the dinghy, rowed ashore and swam from the beach, it was lovely. Next day was a rainy morning and although it cleared by early afternoon I thought I'd stay another day, whats the rush when you are in such beautiful places. It was a lovely bay backed by wooded hills scattered with houses climbing the hillsides, there were a number of beautiful beaches and behind the rest of the ria, always with these beautiful wooded hills. But then it was time to move on so I weighed anchor and set out for the Illas Cies.

There had been a low, sort of stuck off the coast of Portugal for the last fortnight or so which had been giving us either no wind or persistent southerlies. Not so good when you are trying to go south. So after reaching out from the ria it was another beating to windward session again. It all started out so well but then where does this wind suddenly spring from, one minute a lovely 15 to 17 knots then its 20, 25, hold on a minute 30 plus knots - more sail shortening practise. I had wanted to anchor off the islands but it was far too windy and the sea too rough so decided to press on to Baiona, a shame for the islands, rocky and rugged look truly beautiful. Into the Enseadia de Baiona after rounding the Ilas Serralleiras and you wonder what the fuss was all about, a gentle breeze and flat sea. You feel a bit silly with 3 reefs still in the main. So I anchored in the bay along with a dozen or more yachts, obviously a popular spot.

After rain overnight and early morning it later cleared and was a bright and sunny. Blowing old boots mind. I decided to put off a trip ashore until the shops re-opened in the afternoon after siesta around 5. However no sooner than I had inflated the dinghy than the heavens opened and the wind was howling, going ashore did not look an attractive prospect at all.

It seems this low had decided to pay us a visit. The barometer had dropped from 1021 millibars, where it has been hovering for days to 1009. Nothing for it but to hunker down and put our trust in the Manson Supreme anchor.

Indeed it blew and rained all night and the mist and rain clouds were down shrouding the hills around the town and across the ria. Even in these conditions it is a lovely spot. Out to the northwest you can see the rugged

Illas Cies, to the north the headland of Monte Ferro, across the bay the town and beaches of Panxon. There is Baiona itself the houses climbing up the wooded hillside and there is the medieval walls of the Parador Conde do Gondamor on the headland.

4. Into Portuguese waters

"There is nothing - absolutely nothing - half so much worth doing as simply messing about in boats." (Kenneth Grahame)

Well I eventually got away from Biaona after being weather bound for 5 days in which it pretty much rained all the time and blew pretty strong at times. It eventually cleared up late Saturday afternoon. Sunday I was pretty tardy getting started and I hadn't thought I'd be leaving but it looked right so I did. I had a struggle to get the anchor up as it had really dug itself in and eventually came up with about a ton, well it felt that heavy when you've no winch to do the donkey work, of mud on it. I then motored into the marina to fill up with diesel and then away. Clear of the harbour all plain sail was set and we reached out to the cardinal mark clearing the rocks off Cabo Silleiro. Here we turned south, we had left the Rias behind and the coast more or less runs south for a couple of hundred miles.

Almost becalmed for a while past the mark and then a nice northerly breeze kicked in. Instead of keeping on a dead run I decided to sail with the wind a few points off the quarter, that way the foresails stay filled and there is less risk of a gybe, altogether more relaxing. Late in the afternoon saw me cross into Portuguese waters so I swopped the Spanish for the Portuguese courtesy flag flying at the spreaders.

It was dark as I approached Viano de Castello, the first feasible port to stop but the almanac advised against a night entry if swell was running. Also I was not able to spot the red light at the mole so made my mind up to carry on. Its always stressful entering strange ports at night plus it was 3 miles to motor up the river to the marina. The only trouble was the wind deserted me just like the fan had been switched off. There was an impressive display of lightning with both sheet and forked lighting which lit up the whole sky over land. Later we had a fickle breeze from the south. The coast had certainly changed in character since leaving Spain, now it was low and at night appeared as a continuous string of lights as far as the eye could see. As I continued I was a little surprised at the number of boats there were about, some passed quite close, no catnapping tonight I needed to keep a constant watch. Later it started to rain. Daylight found us somewhere off Povoa de Varzim but now the coast was shrouded in mist and rain and the need for tacks every so often I was finding a bit wearing, progress was slow. In the end I decided to motor the last miles as the wind was right on the nose. Leixoes was spotted but it seemed to take forever to reach. But now at least the mist had cleared and the rain lighter and entering the harbour it stopped. Fenders out, lines made ready and I entered the marina. Where to go? the marina staff waved me to a pontoon and helped with my lines. It was midday, so a passage of 24 hours for what the chart says should be 63 nautical miles, but I must have sailed farther with the gybes and tacks. The log was playing up, still under reading, the wretched thing read 53. First things first, a cup of tea and then a nap.

Leixoes is near the mouth of the Rio Douro on which Porto stands, famous of course as the centre for port production. From the bus stop outside the marina I took a bus ride into Porto and had a very interesting walk about the old city, the quayside and the port warehouses. Needless to say a bottle of fine port was purchased.

Out to sea after leaving Leixoes there was a surprisingly large swell, considering how calm the weather. The morning started with gentle southeast winds then later a calm and in the afternoon the wind returned from the northwest gradually getting stronger as the afternoon progressed. I rigged the big red and white cruising chute and when the wind was about 8 knots it was pulling like the proverbial steam train. Later as the wind increased to about 13 knots I decided enough of such nonsense, this would seem like about the upper limit for this huge sail so I handed it. Thanks to it's snuffer a relatively easy task.

The coast here is just an endless line of sand dunes and beaches on which even 2- 3 miles out you can hear the surf roar. Navigation is straightforward, you just get far enough off shore to find the 20 m depth contour and then turn south.

The intention was to enter Ria Averio but the pilot gives dire warnings of the effects of swell so I was a little uncertain whether to attempt an entry but I closed with it to have a look. Some big ships were coming out and some smaller fishing boats too and then I saw a yacht about to enter so I followed at a discreet distance and it turned out there was no problem. I motored up the river and anchored off the little town of St Jacino. The area is one of lagoons, sand dunes and salt marsh but is very developed industrially.

In the morning I headed out through the harbour moles. There was a bad swell breaking to the south so I headed west to clear it, an outgoing small fishing boat also pointed me out the way. Once again out to the 20 m depth contour and turn south for more endless miles of sand dunes and beaches. Early afternoon saw the northwest breeze kick in again so out with the cruising chute. Not far behind me was Jean Michelle and his Wharram cat who I had meet earlier in Spain. They had been catching me until I hoisted the chute but now we could just stay ahead. Past Cabo de Monego I handed the chute and gybed towards the port of Figuera da Foz which I entered and found a berth in the marina for the night.

Yesterday the log had not worked all day so after taking out the paddle wheel and cleaning it I hoped it would be back in business. More of the same sort of coast until the early afternoon when we passed the lighthouse of Penedo da Saudade. Here the coast was a little higher and more rocky in nature. On the whole though it is not an inspiring coast to cruise along.

This afternoon the wind failed so we motored to round Pontal da Nazare and entered the harbour of Nazare where I berthed in the marina.

In the morning the marina staff told me today would be bad weather in the sense of rain, so I was a little undecided whether to stay or press on. I walked into town in the morning which it seems has developed into quite a tourist town but there were still signs of the old way of life with racks of brine soaked fish put out to dry in the sun on the beach. Back at the boat the weather didn't look bad so I left.

About an hour later I wished I hadn't. The sky was black, riven by lightning flashes and there was a torrential rain. From what I could see though it would pass and indeed the worst was over fairly soon and although still overcast the rain was just light. Whilst all this is going on I just sheltered under the spray hood keeping a watch and the boat steers herself, I didn't even get wet.

Later visibility improved and I could see the Os Farihoes, a group of islands off the coast. I was aiming to pass between the mainland, Cabo Carvoeiro and the island of Berlenga.

The weather further improved and I rounded Cabo Carvoeiro in bright sunlight and from there it was just a little way to the port of Peniche. I was moored by 4pm so a nice short day, just a pity that the marina office was closed so no key for the gate. I could have got out of course but not back in. Still I borrowed a card and key from a couple on an English boat which I had seen anchored at Baiona so I could have a shower.

I had a day in Peniche. I had found on deck a washer and a nut, now where on earth did they come from? A check around revealed nothing but ah did the radar reflector mounted up the mast look a little wobbly? So it was up the mast armed with spanners and a new nut and bolt and that was soon fixed. Later sitting outside a bar using their wifi I noticed across the street a restaurant that seemed so popular they were queuing outside. I thought that it must be good so a bit later when the crowds thinned I treated myself to a lavish lunch of grilled swordfish with prawns for starters. Yes it was good.

There was a 16th century citadel in Peniche that had been used more recently for a high security prison for opponents of the dictatorship which was only overthrown in 1974. Now that is recent history to me, a dictatorship in Europe that short time ago. It makes you think and realise just how insular us English are, so ignorant of our European neighbours affairs.

Leaving next morning I was a bit hemmed in on the pontoon with boats close astern and in front. The beamy bugger in front was moored bow in so his broad back end was sticking right out. Time to spring off. A rear spring line, a fender on the stern quarter and motoring astern swung my bow out nicely to clear him.

The first 2 miles away from the harbour or so was a veritable minefield of pot buoys. Further down the coast I passed close to 2 anglers far out in a little rib. One proudly held up 2 huge fish that they had caught. The forecast had promised northerly breezes but I had only a light southerly headwind and the northerlies did not start until late in the afternoon. At one time I had about 8 yacht sails in sight, all on passage south. We passed the impressive Cabo da Roca and shortly after the low lying Cabo Raso. From here I headed into Cascais where I anchored for the night.

It blew quite hard in the night and the morning was windy too but I was in no rush to get away as I was waiting to catch the tide up the Rio Tejo as I had decided to visit Lisbon. It was an interesting sail up the river passing many of the old fortifications. Passing under the suspension bridge I entered the Doca de Alcantara, an old commercial dock where now there is a marina. Plenty of berthing practise today, first at the waiting pontoon for the swing bridge, second on a long pontoon where I left Sea Bear to visit the marina office and thirdly to the berth they allocated me. That last was tight, but I got in OK without hitting anything.

I keep seeing boats that I have seen before, all on their passage south, its like nautical leapfrog. Here it was a big German boat flying a huge ARC2014 flag, on the way to the ARC obviously, last seen in Camarinas. At Cascais it was Jean Michell again in his Wharrram, who I first met in the Ria Cedeira, the big French HR seen at anchor at Bueu and a German aluminium boat also seen in Camarinas.

It was now October. I spent a day in Lisbon walking around in the hot sun. I visited the maritime museum which was worthwhile. Hats off to those early Portuguese navigators exploring in boats that were sometimes not that much bigger than some modern couple's yachts. Lisbon is a fascinating city, huge and sprawling with loads of character summed up by old buildings, cobbled roads and pavements, and tiled buildings. If you liked cities it is the sort of place you could get stuck in. I found a non tourist area and had lunch at a cafe on the street, a sort of mixed fish stew flavoured with fresh coriander and one of the custard tarts, Pastel de Nata, that a friend Matt had told me to look out for.

Passing out through the swing bridge into the Rio Tejo we took the first of the ebb down the river. There were some huge cruise ships moored on the outside of the dock disgorging passengers for their day in Lisbon. The river is really wide so with a gentle following wind I gybed down the river and passed the light of Bugio built on a shoal at the river entrance. The entrance shoals to the south so you have to stand out quite a way to sea to clear it before turning south. Much later we rounded Cabo Espichel with on its south side some dramatic sea cliffs. One of which issued jets of spray from some undersea opening. Off Sesimbra was an anchored Portugese four masted schooner, a lovely sight. Passing into the harbour we anchored off the beach. I don't think I had ever seen so many seagulls in one place before, oh maybe except at Bridlington.

Sesimbra has a reputation for its strong northerly breezes in late evening and at night and that day was no exception.

First light saw us weighing the anchor and away. There were now two schooners anchored outside. From the look of it they were Naval training vessels. The Portuguese are obviously rightly proud of their seafaring tradition and their navy can find the money to run these fine ships. So why can't Britain? Probably because our government choose to spend it on useless high tech weaponry and the Trident nuclear submarines instead.

My route today lay across the wide Canhao (Bay) de Setubal so I was out of sight of the coast mostly and there was not much to see apart from lots of dolphins. Still we had a good sail in the morning with a fine easterly breeze and Sea Bear could stretch her legs on a beam reach.

Cabo de Sines was reached and rounding it and the long breakwater we entered the harbour of Sines and moored up in the marina. Another nice looking town climbing up the hillside and a nice beach.

The next leg was gonna be a long one. It was 56 nautical miles from Sines to Cabo de Sao Vincente, a coast with no intermediate harbours and then another 5 nautical miles or so to an anchorage. It would be touch and go whether I could do the whole thing in daylight, which then was from 7.30 to 19.30. The forecast was for quite strong winds with a 2.7 metre swell and Cabo de Sao Vincente has a reputation for roughish seas so I was in two minds whether to go. On the other hand I needed good winds to stand a chance of making it in daylight.

Out from the shelter of the harbour it was certainly a little rolly, but then you can't have wind without waves. With 1 reef in the main, staysail and a partly furled yankee Sea Bear started to pick up her pace. The dolphins certainly seemed to revel in the conditions and you could see them clearly in the waves appearing to surf them. I watched them for ages from the foredeck whilst sweet Martha looked after the steering. Martha is the self steering gear.

The wind later picked up a little, we had 20 knots apparent wind and since we were running at about 5 to 6 knots the real wind was about 26 knots. Go Sea Bear go. There were lots of white horses and you could hear the roar as their crests broke behind you. Sometimes it is better not to look. Still she is such a good sea boat that we stayed dry, not so much as a splash in the cockpit all day. Late in the afternoon I could see Cabo de Sao Vincente, we were making good time. Of course the last few miles always seem to take ages even though the GPS was recording Sea Bear as touching 7 knots at times. 18.30 saw us almost up with the Cape and Pta de Sabres was starting to open up beyond it. We were in a position were we could gybe towards Pta de Sabres. We were round Cabo de Sao Vincente in daylight and rounding Pta de Sabres dark was failing but there lay the anchorage. It was a question of creeping carefully into the beach in the dark, there was a moon but also clouds. Finally I could let the anchor go in a depth of 9 m off the beach and once assured it was properly set I could relax.

In the morning I could appreciate what a pretty little bay and beach it was. Here we were at the start of the Algarve. Sailing along the coast was spoilt a little by a nightmare of fishing nets. They were all highly visible and well buoyed and so simple to avoid but it meant keeping out by the 50m depth contour and it was a bit far out. It looked such an interesting coast I would have liked to sail closer inshore.

Turning Pointa de Piedade, a lovely stretch of cliffs with pinnacles coves and caves I arrived at Lagos and anchored off the beach. It was mid afternoon but I awarded myself a short day on account of yesterday.

Next day was a gentle sail proceeding slowly past the coast. There were some lovely stretches of cliffs with sea caves and by mid afternoon I moored up inside Albufiera marina.

Albufiera was the full blown complete tourist resort. The marina was surrounded by apartments and the old fishing village completely lost amongst tourist development. The beach was like something out of a holiday brochure, rows of sun loungers with thatched sunshades. The cafes boasted menu touriste and full english breakfast and rows of shops with holiday mementos. It was all rather ghastly.

In the afternoon I waked to a smaller beach or cove with crumbling cliffs and pinnacles. There were still the sun loungers etc but at one end it was quieter so I went for a swim. Later I walked backed along the cliff tops, a nice walk.

Rain and more rain the next day so I took the opportunity to tidy and clean up the boat.

Next morning was raining too, but the forecast was for it to stop raining by 10 and then sunshine. Away from the marina there was a deceptively nasty little swell which threw the boat about all which ways. They were wrong about the sun for it never appeared all day. Eventually we got a little wind and we got to the entrance to the lagoons of Faro and Olhao, which was a couple of stone moles sticking out from the sand dunes. The book warned of a strong tidal set across the entrance and they were not wrong and once between the moles the flood tide accelerated me down the channel. Once the lagoons opened out the tide eased off and I went and anchored in the lee of the island of Culatra. It was a popular anchorage, there was probably 20 or so boats anchored up. The final cap on a not particularly enjoyable day was that the cooker stopping working hallway through cooking tea and despite all my efforts refused to work.

In the morning, having diagnosed the problem with the cooker to be a blocked fuel valve there was nothing for it but to empty the cooker tank and clean everything out. Taking out the tank didn't prove to such a difficult task as I feared. I cleaned the crud from the tank and unblocked the fuel valve and voila I could have my morning cup of tea.

Mindful of the tide experienced through the channel yesterday I planned my departure for low water slack so departure was less stressful. It was another grey and dismal day though and it wasn't long before the rain started accompanied by peals of thunder. This went on all day until about 1 hour short of the entrance to the river Guardiana, when the sun came out for a while. The river marks the border between Portugal and Spain. By the bar buoys I handed the main and ran in over the bar under the yankee alone. Fortuitously I arrived at the marina in Vila Real de Santo Antonio at slack water. The marina is just built stuck out into the river so to speak and the tide runs strongly through it, so berthing at slack water is less traumatic than at other times. Ashore there was a market in full swing so I went for a wander. Pots and pans, crookery, knives, and sheepskin slippers, were the main items on offer but there was a van selling the Portuguese version of hot fresh doughnuts. Later it rained again torrentially.

5. Spain Again

"A bad day sailing is better than a good day at the office." (Anon)

According to the pilot book and people I spoke to, the upper reaches of the Rio Guardiana are not to be missed. Accordingly next afternoon I took the flood tide up the river. Indeed once under the suspension bridge the river side is pretty much unspoilt and sparsely populated. The weather was a little unsettled and at one point I was hit by a 35 knot squall which came out of nowhere. I thought I might end up in the bank but managed to avoid that with a struggle. The squall was of course accompanied by heavy rain so I was drenched in no time, most unpleasant but it was all over in about 20 minutes. Strangely enough a boat about 200 or 300 metres further up the river than me missed this squall completely.

Reaching the tiny village of Foz de Odeitte I anchored and spent a tranquil late afternoon and evening just sitting in the cockpit.

In the morning I had to clear a raft of canes, reeds and small branches that had accumulated around the anchor chain before I could weigh anchor. I then motored and drifted slowly back down the river on the ebb. The sky looked threatening with rain but by dint of getting waterproofs all ready to don I seemed to ward it off.

I entered the marina at Ayamonte, on the Spanish side of the river by a ferry glide manoeuvre as the tide runs strongly past the entrance, but once inside you are completely sheltered. The almost obligatory wander around the town revealed it to be quite charming with tiled plazas. Later the bad weather did arrive, it blew strongly and bucketed it down with rain.

Late afternoon, some nice weather for a change and just a little before low water I ventured away from the marina, down the river and out over the bar. I was glad it wasn't too bumpy as there was not much water under the keel. Once clear I had a fine wind and all plain sail set was off on a beam reach for Cadiz. It was about 65 or so miles so I knew that it would be an all night affair. About 5 miles out I passed over a very marked line where the water colour changed dramatically, it was very striking. A little after sunset and I passed two big ships at anchor, sort of in the middle of nowhere really a good 15 or more miles off the coast. I slid past their bows hoping the sleeping monsters didn't awake and start moving. Until midnight though we were making good time. Then the wind which had been 10 to 15 knots went more westerly and died to about 5 knots then less. I persevered for a while but eventually when our speed was 1 knot and it was 8 miles to the clearwater buoy I succumbed and on went the engine. So eventually I entered the harbour and then the marina and tied up in the first available berth. After a couple of hours sleep I went through the usual rigmarole at the office and moved to another berth. A grey day, rain later. I must say since I had reached the Algarve the weather had not been very good at all.

Cadiz, city of scooters, narrow streets, parakeets nesting in palm trees, people fishing from the city walls, a fantastic fish market. Surrounded on almost all sides by the Atlantic ocean. It's a nice city.

I bought provisions for the boat and checked all the boat over. Joining me here I had crew, a Dutch girl, Merel, so it would help with these longer passages to come. It was time to leave mainland Europe and head further south. We would see if the swell would let us into any of the Moroccan ports.

6. To Morocco

"To young men contemplating a voyage I would say go." (Joshua Slocum)

After topping up with diesel at the fuelling berth we headed out of the harbour and out to the clearwater water buoy at the end of the Canal Norte. Here we could turn southwards and after passing the west cardinal buoy marking the rocks and shoals to the west of the Cadiz peninsular set a course for Rabat some 170 miles away. There was a nasty cross swell so the boats movement was a trifle lively and Merel succumbing to Mal de Mer felt off colour. There was little wind, so progress was slow and eventually resort was made to the engine for an hour. Then the wind picked up, great at first but later after dark it further strengthened leading me to put in first one reef and then later a second reef in the main and furling the yankee. There were quite some waves, one even decided to join me in the cockpit, fortunately an unusual occurrence for Sea Bear.

Later the wind and seas calmed down but then it became foggy, very foggy. I knew there were some fishing boats about as I had seen their lights before the fog and I could hear their engines in the distance. The

AIS told me they were 2 miles off so not too worrying but I slowed the boat down by loosening all the sheets and proceeded cautiously. The fog cleared later to return briefly after daylight. Then we had a nice day sailing, light winds, only 8 to 10 knots but progress on the desired course was being made.

Just before sunset we saw a large pod of dolphins. Another night passed by. There were the lights of numerous fishing boats but none came very close and none for which we had to alter course for. In the early hours we could see the loom of lights on the Moroccan coast, the lights of Mehdiya and further on Rabat.

Dawn and were about 8 miles off Rabat, however then the wind headed us so we had to go on the other tack and then it died completely. In a way this calm did us a favour as instead of slowly tacking our way in we had the perfect excuse to switch on the engine and motor the remaining miles. Off the harbour entrance we radioed the marina for the pilot and although we got no reply the pilot boat appeared and said to wait 1 hour and they would be back when there was enough water to cross the bar. So in due course the pilot boat led us in through the harbour entrance and up the river to the police and customs pontoon. I was glad for the pilot as the entrance was tricky and even what little swell was running made it a little exciting. But oh what an entrance, sailing up the river between two medieval walled towns, you knew you were arriving somewhere very different, was it even this century. There was a huge wow factor.

There was a little snag over our entrance formalities. You see the skipper had overlooked that the boat insurance had expired 2 days ago and we could not proceed into the marina until this had been sorted. They were pleasant enough about it and directed me around to the marina office who again were more than helpful and I could email the insurance company and I later phoned them and they emailed me a new insurance document which the police then printed out for me so it was all sorted in the end, it just took a bit of time, and we could moor up in the marina.

Eh it were a bit warm - 35 degrees in the shade thats in the nineties for us oldies, but I loved it.

In the evening we strolled into the walled city of Sale, we found a hole in the wall which accepted my card and gave me some dirhams and then we wandered through the Medina. After a glass of mint tea from a tea shop we bought some fresh cooked warm maize cakes from one stall and some fried fish with sauce in bread from another stall so dinner was sorted.

Sea Bear, when I bought her, came with a roll of canvas fabric labelled sunshade. It was time to dig it out of the locker and figure out how to rig it. It provided shade in the cockpit and also kept the rest of the boat a little cooler.

The marina is on the Sale side of the river, part of a big new development of apartments so later we walked down to the river and took a ferry boat across to the Rabat side. These are wooden rowing boats which they row standing up facing forwards and ferry glide across the current in the river.

In Rabat we went into the Medina and found a little place to eat with tagines on a hot plate outside. Tagines are a traditional Moroccan shallow earthen ware dish with a conical lid in which are cooked vegetables, onions, tomatoes, olives and potatoes eaten with bread. Very filling, very simple, very tasty.

Medinas all round are a bit of a sensory overload, there is so much going on, so much to hear and see. Clothes stalls, stalls of olives, stalls of spices, colours and smells. Emerging much later we were by the grave yard which lies between the city and the sea -its vast.

We then found our way to the Kasbah des Oudayas a truly delightful walled community and the part that so impressed on our entrance. Lots of narrow winding streets or alleys painted blue lower down and white higher up and with many potted plants.

Descending to sea level we were at the beach, there seemed quite a lively surf scene. More mint tea was taken looking out over the beach. We passed back through the Kasbah, exploring a little more and then eventually took a ferry back to the the Sale side and so back to the boat. A fascinating day with the promise of yet more to explore and see.

Next day was another day of exploring and sightseeing which was also good but once again it was time to move on. I had always had it in mind to arrive in the Canaries by the end of October. It was 450 or so miles to the tip of the nearest northern most island of the Canary Islands, La Graciosa, so I thought it should take from 5 to 8 days depending on the winds.

7. Off to the Canaries

"You can't cross the sea merely by standing and staring at the water."
(Rabindranath Tagore)

After a walk into Sale in the morning to stock up on fresh vegetables and bread, getting clearance from Moroccan customs and police was straightforward. A pleasant customs official gave me an orange to eat. The police did bring along a sniffer dog, a big alsatian, who they persuaded with some difficulty to board the boat. But I must say all the officials we dealt with in Morocco were very polite, helpful and cheerful, not at all officious.

Around 3pm the pilot boat lead us out down the river over the bar and through the outer harbour. We had enjoyed our stay in Morocco. I would heartily recommend a visit, its a crazy lovely place.

There was little wind although the weather site had suggested we would get northerly winds so it was motoring at first. Later a gentle southwesterly breeze filled in and we could sail, but hard on the wind as the coast trends southwest here. Evening found us zigzagging to get past fishing nets. They were buoyed and lit at night and once which end was the landward end and which the seaward end was figured out, didn't pose too much of a problem. There was generally a small open Moroccan fishing boat close at hand and they would shout and wave their arms or flash a light at you if they thought you were going the wrong way.

In our first 24 hour period we logged 71 miles, probably nearer 78 to allow for an under reading log, which was not too bad considering the conditions. Alas it was not to last and for the next few days we were plagued with either light headwinds or calms. The forecast northerlies just never arrived. The writing in the log was a succession of engine on, engine off sailing again, engine on calm, again over and over again. It was a little frustrating at times. It doesn't help when you are plotting your position on a passage chart where the passage distance of 470 miles measures about 330 millimetres so a plot of a 6 hour run consists of 2 pencil marks 12 millimetres apart - it looks so little progress.

You settle into some kind of rhythm as night follows day and without the written log it would be easy to lose track of the days. Having Merel along to share the watches was great help, even though sleep was maximum of 3 hours at a stretch, you didn't get so dog tired and it was good to have someone else besides myself to talk to.

Even on our last full day at sea when we did have a northwest wind, it came in fits and starts but we were getting closer. The last night fell and we had about 50 miles still to go and now the wind did blow and Sea Bear romped along. At around 11pm some lights high on Lanzarote were visible. The only trouble was it now looked liked we would arrive off the north end of Lanzarote in the early hours whilst it was still dark. There are few navigational lights, 1 small lighthouse on Pta Delagade, one of the outlying (uninhabited) islands and the unlit rocky island of Roque del Este. It's not a coast to flirt with in the dark. Some way off then I hove to for an hour or so and when the sky in the east showed signs of lightening let draw again and made for the channel between Lanzarote and Isla Graciosa.

It certainly is a dramatic landfall. We soon reached the little harbour of Caleto de Sebo on Isla Graciosa. However we were told by a security official who after consulting his clipboard and found the name Sea Bear not on his list that the marina was full. Puzzling really as I could see at a glance at least 8 or more vacant berths. Turned away from the harbour we went and anchored in the next bay at 10 in the morning. The setting and scenery were breathtaking but somehow I hadn't expected these desert islands, sand and volcanic cones set here in the ocean.

It has been said of Isla Graciosa.

"When you land on Graciosa you take off your shoes and forget the world"

After anchoring and after lunch it was time to inflate the dinghy and row ashore, landing on a small beach. A short walk along a beach backed by volcanic rocks and desert shrub land took us into the small village of whitewashed single story houses where the streets were just sand. We had a coffee at a little harbour front cafe. We later walked to Playa Francesa, another beautiful bay and anchorage.

Next morning we dinghied into the harbour and spoke with Pedro the "director do porto" who said yes the marina was full but fortunately Merel spoke excellent Spanish and after more talk ah well you can berth either there or there or there! So we moved Sea Bear into the harbour alongside a pontoon, this time we were on the security official's list. This was better as we had discovered yesterday that no-one was allowed to anchor in the bay we were in and the beach where we had landed yesterday was tricky to leave. It was fringed with reefs and I had to launch the dinghy in a shallow lagoon then row out through a small gap, thankful that the waves were not bigger.

There are no paved roads on the island, just dirt tracks. Some mountain bikes were hired and a circuit of the northern part of the island undertaken. A visit to the beautiful Playa de Las Conchos, a walk up Montana Bermeja, the village of Pedro Barber visited and a swim in the bay there. One evening we dined ashore on octopus, sardines and mushrooms with a bottle of wine from Lanzarote - delicious.

Days passed, the island is touched by tourism but only very lightly, it is so laid back, such a relaxing place, a visit there is highly recommended by me.

Eventually we left Graciosa and with a northerly wind of 10 to 13 knots had an uneventful sail around the top of Lanzarote and down the eastern coast. Arriving at Arrecife, the islands capital we entered into Puerto de Naos and there found, instead of just the 2 pontoons mentioned in the pilot, a brand new marina. We discovered that it had only opened on 18th October just 4 weeks ago. There were lots of boats here including many from the Atlantic Odyssey, a new cruise in-company started by Jimmy Cornell.

Arrecife was a bit of a contrast to Graciosa, but with good connections a good place for crew to come and go and a good base to explore the island from. One day we took a bus to Yaiza, a delightful village, and walked and hitched to El Golfo, where there is a striking green lagoon and then along the coast past amazing lava flows. We ended the day with a swim on the beach at Playa

Blanca, a place full of lobster coloured English - we didn't stay long.

It was then time for Merel to leave, she was flying back to Spain. Sad to see her go as she had been great company and we'd had a good time together. She left me with an aloe vera plant and a bottle of Rum as a leaving present, "Cuz real sailors (pirates) don't sail without Rum! Arrrh"

However I wasn't alone for long as Wendy, my best friend from Sheffield, arrived on a plane a few days later. 15 minutes off the plane and we were swimming in the sea at Playa Honda, fabulous. The next week was spent exploring the island, swimming most days and taking in a few tourist sites. These included the house of the artist Cesar Manrique, who had such an influence on the island, the Mirador del Rio, a wonderful viewpoint, Cuevo de Verdes, the lava tube caves and Timanfaya, the fire mountain or Mount Doom as it became where you could feel the heat of the volcano and peer down a fumarole to its depths. Sardines, octopus, prawns were eaten along with various tapas too and the very good Lanzarote wine drunk. But in case you are thinking it was all just good times, work was done too, eye splicing to make up some new halyards for Sea Bear.

Wendy returned to the UK and it was time to move on but a spell of bad weather arrived. We had a number of days of strong winds and rain, at times torrential. It even flooded some of the towns streets.

Eventually I got away from Arrecife. Leaving the pontoon was tricky with a tail and cross wind, but I managed OK. Outside the harbour I set a course for Fuerteventura, downwind sailing this was, so just the yankee and the staysail set and I didn't bother with the main. I also reckoned it would be easier as I was passing through one of the noted wind acceleration zones where the winds are reported to go from 15 to 30 knots in an instant. These wind acceleration zones are caused by the winds funelling between the islands. It was a cloudy day but it passed without event.

I thought I might put into Puerto del Castillo for the night, but off here the sun was about to set, a night approach not recommended so I carried on. There were very few lights ashore on the next stretch of coast, Fuerteventura is indeed a wild and rugged looking island. I rounded the light on Punta de la Enstallada and it was then only 6 miles to Gran Tarajal. Here I anchored in the bay to the east of the breakwater. 55 miles run, quite pleased with my progress.

After weighing anchor next morning my course was along the south coast of Fuerteventura, with northerly winds, a nice beam reach and in the lee of the island flatter seas, a real pleasure. Several boats had emerged from the harbour of Gran Tarajal, most were much bigger so drew away but Sea Bear under full sail did overtake one boat with reefs tucked in. Later I put a reef in the main myself as the wind was picking up. A red letter day, I saw my first flying fish, I was amazed at how far it flew.

We passed the lighthouse on Punta de Mattoral O de Morro Jable and Morro Jable itself. Along this Costa Calme the wind was very variable, calm one moment and 25 knots the next, it kept you on your toes. I anchored at Puertito, a tiny bay and settlement tucked in close by the Punta Jandia, the very bottom tip of Fuerteventura.

First light saw me away again. The surf was most impressive, breaking over the reefs and outlying rock off Punta Jandia. A wide berth was given and the course set for Gran Canaria.

Unfortunately with a northwest wind it was a hard beat instead of a reach. Clear of the lee of the island there was quite a sea. In the afternoon the wind increased and we had 24 - 25 knots increasing to 30 knots at times. It was a struggle to hold the desired course. The stowage in the cabin was, let us say re-arranged. Items which had happily remained in their place for 3 or so months, now decided to move, mostly to the cabin floor. Eventually with the wind right on the nose the last miles were motored. It rained intermittently as well. Safely within Las Pamas harbour I anchored amidst the other boats here.

I must say I didn't really enjoy Las Palmas. I moved into the marina which took over 2 hours waiting, queuing and doing the paperwork. Then I was put in an annexe to the main marina which wasn't very good, it was open to swell so suffered from surge. My first experience of bow too mooring as well, it made getting off and on the boat awkward.

Las Palmas itself so big so busy and just full of traffic and I didn't find it very interesting. There was a big storm day after I moved into the marina and the weather for my stay wasn't too good at all.

Still new crew was taken on, an Austrian lady who reputedly had a yachtmasters qualification, a few jobs were done on the boat and a restock of provisions.

Its hard getting away from these Spanish marinas early, first there is the gate keys to return and get the deposit refunded, then fuel up with diesel, so it was 11am before we were away. Outside of the harbour our way was south, there was a fair old swell so it was a bit rolly. Later the wind picked up further, peaking at 25 to 30 knots so a lively sail. Passed the lighthouse of Maspalomas, and all the sand dunes it was a bit quieter and we tucked into the bay by Pasito Blanco just as the sun was setting and put down the anchor for the night.

Away bright and early but hardly any wind and then none, so on with the engine to motor past the cement factory imaginatively named Puerto Cementero. Here we could alter course, bound for the southern tip of Tenerife and we had some wind, a gentle southwesterly. Before long that deserted us but white horses approaching from the north announced a northeasterly blow. It blew hard all afternoon and mostly all night with a long period of a sustained 30 knots and peaks of 35. We were down to just the staysail and with big breaking seas it wasn't really too much fun. We did have a wonderful view of the snow tipped Teide above the clouds and later had a big full and bright moon. Once under the lee of Tenerife, the sea was not so rough, the wind abated and we could see the lights of La Gomera. Just before dawn we were becalmed, it was just like someone had switched the fan off. The breeze returned fitfully later. As we approached La Gomera we could see what a beautiful and rugged island it was. Eventually just after midday we entered the big breakwater of San Sebastian harbour and thence into the marina for a berth. It looked like this place would be the perfect antidote to Las Palmas.

On the pontoon I ran into Ollie who I had first meet in Ayamonte, he was sailing his Albin Vega from

Scotland to the Caribbean single handed. It was good to meet up again and swap sea tales.

The first afternoon I walked up to the view point over the harbour and then to the lighthouse. I still had my sea legs so the earth kept moving. The town, which is very attractive, is situated where one of the barrancos of the island descends to the sea, there is only a small level area and much of the town climbs steeply up the hillside.

It seemed like my new crew couldn't cope with shorthanded sailing so she jumped ship and I was on my own again.

One day I took a bus to Pajarito and then walked up to Alto de Garajonay, at 1,487m the highest point of the island. There were woods and shrubs, striking volcanic pinnacles and I heard and saw canaries singing in the bushes.

8. Bound for the Cape Verde Islands

"The sea folds away from you like a mystery. You can look and look at it and mystery never leaves it." (Carl Sandberg)

I had almost decided to cross the Atlantic singlehanded but without effort from me I had two potential crew approach with a view to crossing the Atlantic. Both seemed fine so I was faced with a bit of a dilemma as to which to choose. In the end I solved this dilemma by deciding to take both. Bertrand, a French sailor and traveler who had crossed before and Jason, an American who has been walking and cycling around Europe for a few years.

Sea Bear was checked over, more provisions bought. It seemed fitting to be setting out from here. It was this very bay where Columbus set out from in September 1492 with his three ships on his voyage of discovery.

It was now mid December, the hurricane season had ended in the Caribbean and a good time to make a start on an Atlantic crossing. I had decided to go via the Cape Verde islands.

After shopping for fresh veg at the market, filling the tanks with water, some last minute chores and getting some exit stamps from the Canaries in the paperwork we were ready for the off, for the 870 nautical miles to the Cape Verde Islands.

Ollie blew his fog horn from the marina breakwater to give us a send off. Outside of the harbour, sail was set and our initial course followed the coast of La Gomera south so we could appreciate more what a wonderful island this was. Winds were light and variable at first, later clear of the island they picked up and gradually more reefs added so we ended with a triple reefed main and a reefed staysail. Later we were down to just the reefed staysail with 35 knots of wind. This wasn't what the forecast had promised at all. The seas built so motion was quite lively and our novice sailor Jason succumbed to mal de mer so was excused watches until he recovered.

Conditions improved on the 2nd afternoon at sea, Jason was recovering so sat in on mine and Bertrand's watches until he had been shown the ropes and we were confident he could stand watches alone. We then ran a 4 hour watch system, 8-12, 12-4, 4-8. This gave us an 8 hour break between watches so a decent sleep could be had. On this passage we did not rotate watches, I had the 4-8 watch so had both sunset and sunrise at around

6.30 but both watches had periods of dark, whereas the others had one 'dark' watch and one in daylight.

There was not a lot to see, no land, no other ships. After a while you could wonder if the rest of the world still existed but a sighting of a vapour trail from an airplane assured us the world was still there. There was very little bird life, just the occasional small black birds, skimming the waves. I regretted not having a bird book aboard to identify them but thought they might be a sooty petrels. We had a few visits from dolphins and saw turtles and flying fish. One morning we found a flying fish on the deck, it was promptly cleaned and popped into the frying pan to provide a small but very tasty morsel for breakfast. Towing a fishing line was unproductive, we lived in hope but were poor in possession.

On the morning of our 8th day out we were within 30 miles of the Cape Verde Islands, but they remained hidden in the haze. The boat had a fine coating of red dust from the Sahara on the windward side. Later the very tip of Pico du Crux on Santo Antao peaked above the haze and as we drew nearer, things though still very hazy, became a little clearer. We ran down the channel between Santo Antao and Sao Vicente and turned into the bay of Porte Grand where lay Mindelo. Sails handed we were soon moored bow to on a pontoon. 8 days almost to the hour after leaving the Canaries, having reckoned on at least 8 and a half days for the passage I was pleased with this.

On our first night we ate ashore to save our supplies for the crossing but also to sample the local fare. We had sort of paella in a rooftop place where a traditional Cape Verde music band played - there was a strong Senegal and Brazilian influence in the music. The town seemed very relaxed.

I completed immigration and boat paperwork in the morning without too much fuss once I had found the right offices to go to. There didn't seem to be any clear signs on doors.

Lunch was eaten at the market, we had rice and some fried fish very tasty. It was a lively place with all sorts going on, women walking by with big baskets of fruit and veg on their heads. It was very African here. You could see that it is a very poor country, third world you might say, but the people were friendly and smiling. One of the local dishes is 'cachupa' which is some sort of cooked grains, another staple is rice and beans and fish of course when available.

Christmas, well was different, no roast chicken and all the trimmings but we did have Christmas pudding which I had stashed in the food locker, plus custard of course. A culinary first for both of my crew.

In the evening the town was really hopping, they had set up a sound system in a square near the beach, so music, people milling about all ages even the tiny tots dancing. It seemed like the whole town was parading about the streets, it was a nice atmosphere.

Friday morning I went to the maritime police and immigration to have the boat and us cleared for exit, as the offices were closed over the weekend. All being well with the meteo, we planned to set off for the Atlantic crossing to Barbados 2000 miles away.

9. Atlantic Crossing

"Crossing oceans under sail is rarely comfortable, but it is always very satisfying." (Eric Hiscock)

We departed Mindelo in the early afternoon of Saturday, after a visit to the market for fruit and vegetables and filling the boats tanks with water. Heading south down the channel it was a little hazy and the island of Santo Antao was not visible although only 5 miles away, conditions not unusual for the Cape Verde Islands. Out of the channel we continued south for some miles so that when turning westward we would not be affected by a wind shadow from the mountains of Santo Antao.

We soon settled in to the routine of watches, deciding on 3 hour watches this time so they would naturally rotate.

I tried my hand at celestial navigation and managed to take some sun sights but got bogged down in the maths of trying to work out a position from them, I didn't really understand it yet. A noon sight was more successful, I found them easier to work out but they only give you latitude, but I came out with a latitude pretty close to our position so decided to keep practising.

We trolled a fishing line and were successful on our second day out, catching a fine dorado which gave us a tasty dinner and ceviche for lunch the next day. Most mornings there were one or two flying fish on deck, 4 was the best haul one morning, eaten for lunch.

Despite a good forecast for the passage, after a couple of days the skies clouded over, it remained cloudy for much of the time after that. The wind was stronger than I had been led to believe of the Trades. 20 to 25 knots apparent and with big seas and a cross swell making the seas quite lively so the motion in the boat made life quite tiring. At one point we were reduced to running under just a storm staysail with apparent winds of over 30 knots. This was definitely not trade wind sailing like the glossy brochures had suggested of blue skies, fluffy white clouds and winds of 15 knots. Even when that first nasty patch of weather passed we had frequent rain squalls with the wind gusting to 30 knots and more. This slowed progress as you would spot the squall, and reef down but there was a certain reluctance to increase sail again too soon after a squall had passed as sometimes there was another hard on its heels. Particularly at night, with squalls hard to spot we would leave the boat well reefed down so we were not always making best boat speed. I was wondering at this point which particular god or gods we had offended so badly, and we hadn't even left on a Friday!

There is an old superstition that one shouldn't set out on a sea voyage on a Friday. It is unsure how or why this superstition originated but some old sea dogs strongly believe that setting off on a Friday will bring bad luck. Ah well those that go adventuring mustn't expect too much in the way of comfort and we were making good progress.

On New Years eve we had a tot of rum to celebrate the new year. 5 days out from Mindelo and we had run just over 500 miles.

On the sixth day out we spotted three, I think whales, too big to be dolphins, astern surfing down a following wave. Lovely but gone of course before a camera came to hand. Very early the next morning we were rewarded with a moonbow or lunar rainbow which is I believe a fairly rare occurrence so I felt privileged to see one. We also caught our second dorado of the trip.

Most of the time we were running under a reefed main often with three reefs in, with staysail and partly furled yankee with the wind on the quarter. We tried to run more downwind with a poled out yankee but with the confused sea state we experienced the rolling was horrendous and the risk of an unintended gybe far too high, even with a gybe preventer rigged.

7 days out and we had run 740 miles so about one third of the way. The weather was remaining unsettled, some nice spells then it became cloudy and with some showers, mostly they were quite light but some were heavy. We took advantage of these by stripping off naked in the cockpit and having a welcome rinse down.

10 days out, we were just over halfway in term in terms of distance, celebrated with another tot of rum.

We passed through lots of floating yellowish seaweed, all seemingly arranged in long orderly lines, quite strange, I since discovered it was sargasso weed.

There was very little signs of life out in mid-atlantic apart from the flying fish. The flying fish were wonderful to watch though, they flew for such a long way and not just in a straight line but twist and turn between the waves, sometime bouncing of the face of a wave to continue their flight rather like a skimming stone.

There were very few birds, the occasional tropic bird with a distinctive long straw like tail, what might be a black capped petrel and maybe a sooty shearwater. Once again I regretted not having a bird book "sea birds of the oceans", if such a one exists, to be able to identify them.

The 13th day at sea and the GPS and chart were telling me that it was 850 miles to Barbados so we were getting there bit by bit. It had been raining on and off for a few days now, sometimes it stopped for a while but it had been grey and damp for days and we hadn't seen the sun in ages. We seemed to have had a bit of a tropical storm, high winds, big seas, for a long time we were running just under a storm staysail, the first time that has been out of its bag, with 30 knots of apparent wind, so real wind was probably 35 knots. You are not supposed to get conditions like this here at this time of year, it was a little worrying at times.

15 days out - 530 miles to Barbados. The weather was still unsettled with fairly frequent squalls. We also had a period of non-stop rain for about 7- 8 hours. I had intended to make landfall in Barbados but I decided it was more sensible to make for Martinique instead especially since from Barbados it was my intention to head north up to Martinique anyway.

Sea Bear continued to run off her 100 miles per day, sometimes a bit less, sometimes a bit more. Gradually the weather improved, there were still a few rain showers from time to time but we were also seeing the sun, a vast improvement, much more like the real thing.

I had to spend couple of hours fixing the heads one afternoon as it seemed to be slowly siphoning clean water back in - I was glad it was clean water! Awkward and cramped it was being tossed around dismantling and reassembling the pump and I ended up in a foul humour I must say.

The fresh vegetables were about finished apart from onions, garlic, potatoes some limes and the last bit of white cabbage so it was down to tinned stuff. The crew were quite inventive with what food stores we had so had ate well so far, if at times strange and bizarre combinations.

There was still much seaweed floating by, it rather spoiled the fishing as it got snagged on the line and hook, you only had too troll the line for a few minutes and oh look another fine catch of seaweed. No good at all when you want fish.

For the last days of our passage we had, sunshine, blue skies and fluffy white clouds and the seas were not so big with winds of between 10 to 16 knots, much more like the trades.

20 days out and there were just under 100 miles to Martinque, we were all looking forward to arriving.

In the early hours of the morning, on our last night at sea we could see the lights of Martinique and with first light, there lay the coast, perfect timing for a landfall. With the wind falling lighter we even dug out and rigged the big cruising chute for the last few miles.

We handed the chute approaching the channel for Le Marin and piloted our way into the anchorage. So many boats after seeing only 3 freighters for the whole passage. We eventually found a clear spot to anchor, hook down, we had arrived. 21 days out from Mindelo 1,111 miles logged, Sea Bear had crossed the Atlantic.

After anchoring at Le Marin, I think it took a while for it to really sink in that we were here in the Caribbean. Firsts things first, after a cup of tea, of course, sail covers on, take off the staysail, tidy up all the ropes, dig out and rig the sun awning. Then it was inflate the dinghy and time to go ashore. We found the dinghy dock and the customs office, but that was closed until Monday. We then wandered along the beach road to the beach where we found a welcoming bar, fresh fruit drinks went down well than to celebrate a t-punch. It was wonderful just to sit there and let it all wash over you, the people, the sights, the sounds, the smells after so long at sea and let it gradually sink in.

Later on we found the supermarket that was open, wine and baguettes and cheese were bought for a picnic on the beach and I found the shower block in the new marina, spirited my way in when someone came out and despite not having a towel or soap had a delightful shower to wash off all the salty spray.

Later that evening there was some bands playing on a stage set up near the beach, good music too.

Next day a patrolling customs rib paid us a visit and decided to search the boat. I was flying the yellow Q flag as required plus the French courtesy flag but they seemed puzzled with the Jack at the stern and the Stars and Stripes flown from the other spreader as courtesy to our American crew. Perhaps we looked a bit dodgy to them. Merde, an Englishman, a Frenchman and an American all on the same boat!

I ended up staying at La Marin a few days, it was nice just to rest up to be on the boat that was secure at anchor and not moving around all the time. I took the staysail to the sail loft as the topmost eyelet for the piston hank had corroded away and there was a little bit of chafe on the leech despite looking out for potential chafe points ever day, but on a black night they can be hard to spot.

The crew departed, Bertrand wanted to remain in Martinique and I felt the need to reclaim some personal space, it had been a long time coped up together in a small boat.

Olly on Solage arrived via Barbados, his first comment to me was *"Its a long way isn't it"*, to which I whole heartedly agreed.

After getting back the staysail from the sail loft and reprovisioning at the nearest supermarket which had a dinghy dock - very civilised, I was ready to leave.

I had a very pleasant gentle sail past Diamond rock and round to the west coast where I anchored in the bay of Grand Anse. Oh what a lovely place this was, a beautiful bay with water so clear you could see the bottom at anchor in 5 meters. Starfish on the sand, fish swimming by, I even saw turtles, amazing. The tidal range here is only about 2 feet so no worries on that score. There was a golden sand beach, some palm trees all backed by lovely wooded hills and some beach restaurants and shacks. Oh the water was such a lovely temperature for swimming. Perhaps this was as close to paradise as I will get.

Next day I walked up and over the headland to the next bay, Petite Anse, I saw a hummingbird, swam, walked back and ate lunch of grilled fish creole style. I would have stayed longer here but I had this date to get to Antigua for so I left the next afternoon for the short hop to Fort De France. Coming into the anchorage I found myself in the midst of Yole race so had my work cut out to keep out of all their way. They sure know how to party do Martiniques, there was a stage set up in the park by the beach and bands playing that evening, for free of course.

I had intended to stay just the one night but the following day it was blowing pretty hard, plenty of white horses out in the bay so I stayed, took the opportunity to wander the streets a bit, swim from the beach.

Next day I sailed to St Pierre, the town that was wiped out in 1902 by the eruption of the volcano Mt Pele. This was a suitable jumping off point for continuing north, next stop Dominica.

10. Cruising through the Leeward Isles

"Twenty years from now you will be more disappointed in the things that you didn't do than in the ones you did do. So throw off the bow lines. Sail away from the safe harbor. Catch the trade winds in your sails. Explore. Dream. Discover." (Mark Twain)

It was now February and next evening I was sitting in Sea Bear at anchor off Roseau, Dominica, she was rocking gently and there were sounds of reggae music drifting out to us across the water. I'd just finished a GandT after dinner. We had made a good passage from St Pierre, Martinique. I'd left with just the faintest glimmer of dawn light in the sky to make sure of getting to Dominica before dark, but we had a really fast passage. Mostly the wind between 15 and 17 knots on the beam, conditions Sea Bear seems to really like, all plain sail set until we took a reef in the main when some gusts pushed 20 knots. For the first time since leaving UK the log was showing an average speed of over 5 knots, in fact 5.5 at one point so we did the passage of 38 n miles in 8 hours, I was really pleased with that.

After anchoring I dinghied ashore and walked to customs to do the paperwork. Quite painless and quick and I liked the clearance document they gave me:

"Commonwealth of Dominica, port of Roseau. This is to certify to all whom it doth concern that Chris Ayres, Master and Commander of Sea Bear burden of 5.89 tons, GRP built and bound for Les Saintes, Guadeloupe having on board ships stores hath here entered and cleared his said vessel according to law."

After clearance I wandered around town a bit, very different to Martinique, which is very French. This was very, well, Dominican and in a way kinda much more of what you suspect the Caribbean to be like if you have never been. Instead of French supermarkets, boulangeries and cafes, there were little grocery stores, all sorts of little shacks and shops, roads with big open gutters, pavements which are broken and uneven and all different materials. It was more like life in the raw.

The island is more mountainous too with lusher vegetation, it's all a riot of colour too, the greens of the trees and vegetation and brightly painted houses and shacks. There were clouds over the mountains and rain showers and beautiful rainbows over the tropical forests.

The people are different too, there are more guys with dreadlocks for instance and it helps that English is the language.

I decided would be a pity not to see some of the interior of Dominica so hailed Pancho as he went past one morning, he was one of the good boat boys and asked about organising a trip. As it happened, two other couples, one French Canadian, the other English were about to go and could do with another person to make up the numbers, so I hopped aboard Pancho's boat and off we went. Anyway all aboard a minibus and off, a lovely drive up into the mountains, first to a waterfall in the national park, in steep tropical forest in the mountains and we bathed in the pool under the falls, then another waterfall and pool, both a bit of walking through the forest which is quite incredible. A spot of lunch at a roadside eating spot, baked chicken drumsticks and fried plantain, then to a beach at Soufriere. Here volcanic gases bubble up through the sand and heat up the sand and the water, hence bubble beach. Ooh and I saw pelicans too for the first time in the wild.

Moving to Portsmouth, Dominica, I anchored in Prince Rupert's bay. I had read bad things about the Portsmouth boat boys but they were good. They had formed an organisation and seemed a nice bunch of guys. Always very polite, friendly and helpful, very careful not to bang their boats into yours. I bought some of the sweetest juiciest grapefruits that I have ever had from Christian in his little rowing boat, very welcome after a hot sail up the coast.

Well I might have said that the Martiniques know how to party, I can only say Dominicans do it more so! Music drifting out over the bay all night until about seven in the morning, and carnival not started yet, it would start Sunday apparently, guess they were just having a Friday night warm up!

I took a trip up the Indian river, by rowing boat, only those are allowed, no outboards etc, because its a national park site. Thick with jungle type trees and coconut palms and lianas. It's where they filmed part of Pirates of the Caribbean, when they went up the river into the jungle, it was a good little trip. I shared a boat with the English couple and their two kids who I meet the other day and went to the waterfalls etc with.

In the evening the Portsmouth boat boys aka PAYS put on a beach barbecue for all the sailors, plenty of rum punch, chicken legs, grilled fish, rice and salad and of course loud reggae music.

Carnival started, the small town of Portsmouth was packed with crowds lining the streets, music blaring out and beer and punch drinking and then came along the procession. The biggest loudest sound systems I have ever see or heard, dancing girls, beauty queens, stilt walkers and then a band. There was dancing in the street, people having fun, all rather wonderful.

I had really enjoyed my stay in Dominica, only my deadline for being on Antigua stopped me from staying longer and doing more exploring of the interior.

There had been rain overnight, but it had cleared by early morning when I raised the anchor at Portsmouth and headed out towards the Dominican channel. There was a light breeze at first which strengthened to between 15 to 18 knots. Sea Bear romped along and just over 3 hours later we entered the Passage du Sud-Ouest and passed between the rocks of les Augustins and the island of Terre-de-Bas of Les Saintes. Here the wind was gusting to 25 knots so we were down to 2 reefs in the main and the staysail. Soon enough though we were picking up a mooring buoy in Anse de Bourg on Terre-de-Haute. Fortunately another boater saw my first attempt to pass a line through the ring thwarted by an untimely gust of wind and hopped in his tender and helped me secure my line. Many thanks to that man.

Formalities ashore soon completed thanks to the computerised French system, you just fill in your details yourself, print out the form, sign it and get them to countersign it.

The town is very pretty but almost overrun by tourists who visit via the fast ferry from Guadeloupe.

Next morning I walked over to Baie de Pt Pierre for a swim, this was a beautiful sandy beach with coconut palm trees. It's also one of the beaches that turtles come ashore to lay their eggs. No sign of them of course, they do it at night.

I crossed the next day to Guadeloupe itself. Coming past the top of Ilet a Cabrit I had to watch out for the fishermen setting some nets. Done with their fast santoises but they amaze me by swimming alongside the nets, something I also saw in Dominica. Bear in mind too this is open water with sizeable waves a mile or so offshore.

With a lovely fresh beam wind I saw the log record a speed of 7.6 knots at one point, very good going for little old Sea Bear. Past the lighthouse on Pte du Vieux Fort, the wind fell light and the seas flatter until eventually faced with a flat calm I resorted to some motoring, then sailing then motoring. Eventually we dropped the hook in Anse de la Barque, a nice little cove with a palm fringed beach but apart from the road passing by nothing else. I took a swim around the boat. In the past I had never been much of a swimmer so bold for me this swimming when I am out of my depth.

Carrying on up the coast next day we passed Bouillante, with it's plumes of steam and then Pigeon island, which is Reserve Cousteau, a marine reserve. I arrived at Anse Deshaies and anchored. A nice little place, a dinghy dock, some beachfront restaurants a few shops, oh and home of Madame Sorbet who sells delicious homemade ice cream from the back of her van in the afternoons. Saw more turtles swimming in the bay here.

For whatever reason I didn't sleep well, so since I was awake at 4am I thought I might as well leave. I had wanted an early start to make sure that I made the 40 mile plus crossing to Antigua and arrive by early afternoon, but didn't mean this early, first light I thought. Anyway the moon was up and stars in the sky, so I stowed the dinghy, hoisted the main and left. There was a gentle breeze which gradually freshened as I made my way away from the coast. I wanted a bit of offing to avoid the headland to the north, the shallow patches and the offshore island of Kahouannp

Later I began to doubt my wisdom, the sky had clouded over and in the half light pre-dawn it looked rather ominous, thought I might get rain squalls but in the distance it looked clearer. In the end I missed all the rain, although I could see it falling on Guadeloupe behind me and gradually the clouds passed and it was another sunny day in paradise. I could get to like this trade wind sailing, a steady northeast breeze between 12 and 15 knots so with the course desired the apparent wind was around 60 degrees, a close reach and with very little swell our speed was good.

Away on our port beam was Monserrat and with the aid of binoculars you could see the ash flows from the eruption of 20 years ago which had caused the evacuation of the island. Ahead were the hills of Antigua, at first looking like a group of separate islands but as we drew closer they merged into one coherent mass. Closer still and I could identify parts of the coast, that surely was Cape Shirley and to its left the Pillars of Hercules marking the entrance to English harbour. Off Snapper Point I handed the sails and motored in between Charlotte Point and Berkley Point to arrive at Freemans Bay, English Harbour. The anchorage was pretty crowded but I found a spot to drop the hook, made the obligatory cup of tea and then sat in the cockpit taking it all in. After all these months I had arrived at my destination, tired but very happy and looking forward to Wendy's arrival.

I spent 5 weeks in Antigua. When I arrived high on the agenda was the need for a bimini. The sun shades I had were all very well for when at anchor but some shade whilst sailing was desirable. A visit to AF Sails set the process in motion, a process that took some time but eventually Sea Bear was fitted with a bimini and so shade whilst sailing, it made a lot of difference to comfort in the cockpit.

Wendy, who provided delightful company, flew out to join me for a month.

Plans to do a little Island hopping were shelved as we had unusually strong winds, days of constant 25 plus knots of wind and higher and at times a rough sea state. There was been plenty to do nonetheless, some delightful anchorages and bays to visit, mainly on the west side of the island, Carlisle bay , Hermitage Bay, Five Islands, Deepbay, Dickenson's Bay, Turners beach and Jolly Harbour but also in the North, navigating through the reefs to anchor off Jumby Bay, Great Bird Island. A beautiful deserted island this, where we saw turtles, stingrays, lizards, hermit crabs, tropic birds, frigate birds and more. Beaches to swim from and walk along. Walks over Middle ground, to Shirley heights and up Fig Tree Drive. Reggae music drifting out at time across the water. A bus ride across the island to St Johns for the markets and lunch in the Palm Court Restaurant, sounds grand but in fact a small local eatery with Creole style food. Fish and lobster meals in beach side restaurants. It was all been pretty perfect really, the people were friendly and helpful, the sea a most amazing turquoise and such a perfect temperature for swimming, the sunsets wonderful.

Once Wendy had left to fly back to England it was time to leave Antigua. I got clearance from customs and immigration at Jolly Harbour and after settling marina fees I reversed Sea Bear out of the berth, always an interesting exercise in a long keeler and went and anchored outside the harbour ready for an early departure in the morning. The weather had reverted to norm now, wind about 15 knots rather than the 25's we had been having and next day I had an uneventful passage to Monserrat where I anchored in Little Bay. Ashore I completed entrance formalities and realised I was a day late for the St Patricks day celebrations. Many of the early settlers were Irish and the tradition is still strong and Guinness is drank in the bars.

A swell was finding its way into the anchorage so the night was not peaceful but anyway next morning I went ashore determined to explore the island. I walked up to the main road intending to take a bus but got offered a lift by someone who had seen me land. On the way he told me something of the island and the changes caused by the volcanic eruptions. He wasn't going all the way to Salem but stopped another car who he reckoned was going there and they gave me a lift the rest of the way, good kind, friendly people on this island.

At Salem I walked up to the volcano observatory, an interesting little walk in its own right arriving at a fine viewpoint of the volcano and the ruins of Plymouth in the distance. That is all still in an exclusion zone as the volcano is still quite active. I walked some way back towards Little Bay, but at a fork in the road, no signposts of course I sat and waited for the bus. They are a good way to see something of the island. It is mountainous and very forested with plenty of wildlife. Only a bit of a nag about the safety of the boat made me return to Little Bay. There, seeing the boat OK, I had a lunch of fried fish at a beach front bar, a beer and an interesting chat with some locals.

I would have stayed longer in Monserrat but the anchorage was so uncomfortable, very rolly and the noise of the crashing surf disconcerting. I had spent two virtually sleepless nights so it was time to go. A shame as I liked the island, mountainous and very forested with lots of wildlife, the pace of life seemed slower too a lovely place. Someday I may go back there and find better anchoring conditions.

The course to Nevis passed close by Redonna, an uninhabited rocky island and reckon I must be getting a bit soft or something. I couldn't see how they would have landed let alone got up the cliffs to mine the phosphate and build a post office! its so steep and looks so loose.

I had a good passage and picked up a mooring in the afternoon at Pinney's beach, just past Charlestown the capital. Lovely peaceful conditions and a good restful sleep was had.

Formalities completed the next morning and a look around Charlestown, a small little place. I went to lookup a fellow member of the Vancouver Organisation, Mark who lives on the Island, has a Vancouver 32 Pearl of Nevis and owns a bar/restaurant on Pinney's beach. He made me very welcome I must say.

Nevis was a nice place to stay, the beach is superb the swimming idyllic and the forest quite wild. I went for a walk hoping I might get to the top of Nevis Peak but the trail just petered out high up in the forest and it would have been all too easy to get lost if I pressed on. Mind you I did see monkeys which was good. Also at Pinney's Beach is the renowned Sunshine's bar and grill. All painted up in Jamaican/Reggae colours, music pumping out and serving the famous Killerbee punch - care needed! Normally returning to the boat from the beach meant launching the dinghy out through the gentle surf. No problem, wade out a bit. Pushing the dinghy to get it afloat and one more shove to get some momentum then leap in and set to rowing. Somehow it all went wrong and I found myself sitting in the surf, soaked and covered in sand, slightly bemused.

I caught a bus up to Qualie beach which is at north end of the island, where I hired a bike and then rode right around the island. It is lovely with some bits like Herbert's beach just fantastically beautiful - it doesn't sound with that name like it should be do it? But it is completely undeveloped, open to, but protected from the Atlantic by a reef. Very few houses at all in this part of the island. The book said the roads are relatively flat for cycling, but the writer of the book has obviously never cycled around the island. There was a big hill, Zion on the road up to Gingerland. That was hard work in the hot sun but of course a lovely run down the other side back to Charlestown. Here I dropped in at the agricultural show - lots of stalls there so I had a good meal of rice and beans, veg and baked chicken and lovely refreshing home made lemonade. Got a puncture going to Fort Charles, which was a bit of a drag but the bike had a spare tube and pump. The owner of bike hire shop, Winston was lovely happy guy and he gave me a lift back to Pinney's beach. A swim soon washed off the sweat from the ride, probably eased the legs too.

After a few more days of relaxing, swimming, it was time to move on again. A short sail took me to Basseterre on St Kitts. Anchored off the town, it was very rolly and uncomfortable but I went ashore for a quick look around, it will repay a further visit. I left there that same afternoon and went across to the southern peninsular of the island, about 5 miles, to anchor in White House bay. Very little there, very peaceful.

The whole southern end of the Island has been bought by a rich American developer who wanted to, has already started to dredge the salt pond for super yacht berths, build a golf course, expensive restaurants, lots of condos all that sort of thing in what was a virtually deserted and unspoilt part of the island. Doubtless it will be all done in good taste but another bit of wilderness gone for good.

A few days with plenty of swimming and short walks ashore. I did visit Basseterre again but with bad timing as it was Good Friday and the place was virtually shut down, it is all too easy to loose track of time.

At White House Bay I meet another Brit, Terry on a lovely 37 ft double ender, we dined on each other boats and talked of this and that. It was nice.

Once more though perhaps it was time to move on, it was already April and there were so many islands still to see. Towards the end of the month I had to be thinking of heading south, out of the hurricane zone.

The morning I left St Kitts, Terry came aboard, gave me a St Kitts cap and a book, and we motored, it being calm, the 2 miles to Frigate Bay where we anchored. Terry thought I should experience a breakfast at Shiggy

Shack, so we went ashore and had the full monty, that is full English breakfast. Seemed a bit incongruous eating a full breakfast on a Caribbean beach. It was my first cooked breakfast for maybe 8 months and I hadn't missed them but this was nice for a change and proper set me up for the day.

Back at the boat I had a gentle breeze so made sail northwards along the St Kitts coastline. I hope I'll go back some day to see more of this lovely island. Departing from the northern tip we had calm for a while but then the breeze was back and the shortish passage to Statia was made. The proper name for the island is St Eustatius but the locals call it Statia. Arriving off Oranjestad, the main town and port I anchored off the beach. It seemed that Easter holidays were in full swing as lined along the beach under the cliffs were sound systems, bands, barbecues, kids on the beach. They certainly like their partying do the Statians.

Ashore next day all seemed to be shut up, the Port Office and the National Park Office so I couldn't complete formalities. I decided to walk up the volcano, called the Quill which dominates the town, you are supposed to buy a hiking permit but as the offices were shut I decided to go anyway.

The way up from the old town, situated on a narrow strip between the beach and the cliffs, mostly destroyed since its heyday in the 18th century, was up the old paved slave road which led from the beach up to the old slave market on top of the cliffs. One wonders what would lead western society to treat Africans in this way, and we called ourselves civilised.!!!!

Passing through the outskirts of the town there was a huge tortoise in someones front garden, must have been a foot and a half long. Higher the track led through woodland, here were purple clawed hermit crabs, they used large snail shells for homes. We are used to thinking of crabs as seaside creatures not 800 ft up a mountain. Arriving at the crater rim you could look down into the crater itself which is full of forest, silk cotton trees and strangler figs. Here too was a feral rooster and feral chickens, one rooster followed me to the rim, quite a bold beast he would eat out of your hand. I went some way down into the crater but the thought of the climb back out deterred me from going too far, beside I had left my full water bottle on the boat and was feeling a little parched. There were lots of little geckos too but I did not spot one of the Statia iguanas.

Back at the beach the party was just warming up again and in the evening things were really hopping. The sound systems all blaring out vying with the bands and the motor bike boys revving their 1000cc bikes up to the full. Mind you there are not that many roads for a burn up on an island that is 4 miles long and 2 miles wide. Crazy crazy Statia, a lovely gem of an island.

The passage to St Barts was not enjoyable. I left the anchorage at Statia early and thought I would go around the south of the island as it would give me a better slant on the wind to cross to St Barts. However tacking around the south of the island proved just too hard, the winds too strong and waves big so after hour and half I had made little progress. I turned around and was back level with the anchorage in 15 mins! so up to the north tip of the island then across. A course almost hard on the wind should have seen me across, unlike the passage notes in the pilot that suggest it should be an easy reach. What with leeway, the current and the waves all pushing me northwards it was soon obvious that I would have to go hard on the wind. The waves seemed unusually large considering the wind strength, just about 18 - 20 knots, sometimes a bit lower and arrangements down below got re-arranged, with stuff all over the cabin floor. As it was I ended up motoring the last miles as I had been headed by the wind and it turned into a race against the sunset, punching into short steep waves with spray everywhere. It was the sort of passage that makes you wonder why you sail at all! Oh and the sunset just won, so I anchored in the dark. Not too bad though, channel buoy lights and other boats at anchor provided some illumination.

Here I was back on the mainstream cruising circuit and there were hundreds of boats. Unlike Monserrat, Nevis, St Kitts and Statia where there were relatively few yachts about.

I'd had to anchor some way out and so it was a long dinghy ride into Gustavia to complete entrance formalities. It feels more like the Mediterranean here than the Caribbean, there seemed a surprising lack of black faces, the population seemed European, its very French, very smart, very chic and expensive too. 5 Euros for a coffee. After a couple of day I moved just a few miles up the coast to Anse du Colombier. This was much nicer, a very lovely bay with turtles swimming about and a gorgeous beach. I walked along a nice coastal path to Anse de Flamades, saw lizards and iguanas. Back at the boat I spent some time diving under the boat scrubbing the bottom watched by some attractive fish.

An easy downwind sail passing between the island of Ile Fourche and the rocks of the Groupers took me to Sint Maarten. In coastal waters here past Great Bay the water was a beautiful turquoise but I was still finding it a little unnerving after all these months in the Caribbean seeing the bottom so clearly even at 20 meters depth.

Anchoring in Simpson Bay I dinghied in to complete formalities. The guy behind me in the queue was a bit pushy and got a good telling off from the lady official, good one lady.

Next day I moved in through the opening bridge to the Lagoon, I fancied a quieter anchorage away from the constant ocean swell where I could get some jobs done more easily. Perhaps the best chandleries in the whole Caribbean are here. One job was to fit a stereo, ipods are all very well but the music I wanted to listen to never seemed to be on the ipod. The stereo I fitted could play the radio, music from ipod and also music from a usb device so I could have access to my entire collection - great.

The other job was to complete the hull cleaning, with being in the water a full year now there was a certain fuzziness to the bottom. I rigged a rope under the boat fastened off side to side by the stanchions and with its aid could dive under the boat and bracing my feet against the keel, scrape off the bottom. It cleaned off easily, the only trouble was there is only so much you can scrape with one lung full of air so it took some time and was quite tiring. From time to time the rope had to be repositioned but eventually after several session it was done.

The island is split between the Dutch half, Sint Maarten and the French half, Saint Marten but you wouldn't really know there was a border between the two. I didn't much care for the Dutch side of the island at Simpson bay somehow, all ribbon development along the busy roads, so I went around to the French side and anchored off Marigot. Seemed a nice little town this, I could have stayed longer but I had it in my head that it was time to turn around and head south. The forecast for the next week was good, lighter winds and easterlies, looked ideal.

11. Heading South to Trinidad

"We are as near to heaven by sea as by land." (Sir Humphrey Gilbert)

I knew it would be an uphill struggle to get back against the wind to St Barts, but I didn't quite figure that it would take all day, hard on the wind, lots of tacking and a wind and sea state that belied the forecast. However I got back to Anse du Colombier before sunset and picked up a mooring in time for a swim. That was good after a hard day.

First light the next day I slipped the mooring bound for St Kitts, I knew it would be another long day. Close hauled I could hold the desired course and I rounded the north end of the island in good time but then a long succession of beats down the coast took ages until a race against the setting sun took me to White House Bay to anchor.

Monserrat was the next destination, first I had to sail past Nevis then it was hard on the wind, 20-25 knots of it - what was this about light winds in the forecast? and there was some south in the wind too so with that and punching into the waves I couldn't hold the desired course. I had thought of anchoring off Little Bay but was pushed too far south and in the late afternoon a quick mental calculation of miles to go with tacking and time before sunset it was apparent that I wouldn't make it. The course I was on would clear the south of the island so be it, a night passage to Guadeloupe it would be. I did give me a fairly close look at the ruins of Plymouth destroyed by the volcanic eruption 20 years ago and yes the volcano was still smoking after all these years.

It was a long night, catnapping was difficult due to the number of ships about, none came close but I like to keep tabs on them. I had shortened sail before dark - it was blowing 25 knots mind, preferring comfort to speed but probably overdid it and when the winds eased later perhaps I should have set more sail. It was a slow passage and dawn found me still miles away from Guadeloupe. Things were not helped by rain squalls which blotted out all visibility. I had though to make for and anchor at Deshaies but had been pushed too far south so settled for making for the Pigeon Islands and anchored in the bay there in the early afternoon. Time for a nap. Waking I wasn't quite happy with the anchorage here, the wind was shifty, swinging room was limited by other boats and holding not too great so I upped anchor and moved 5 miles down the coast to

Anse du Barque - much better and I had a very peaceful night there.

Raising anchor the next morning was hard as in the boat swinging the chain seemed to have wrapped itself around a rock but eventually I got it up and was off. But what was this southerly wind of 20 knots and I wanted to go south down the coast. I am never ever going to believe in weather forecasts ever again. It had been wrong every day. Plan A had been to make it to Dominica, I scrapped that to go to Les Saintes instead, this lies further east so more tacking but not so far and from there should give a better slant on the wind for Dominica. Plenty of vacant moorings in Bourge les Saintes.

I remained there the next day, it was cloudy with rain but I fancied a stretching my legs ashore. I walked up to Fort Napoleon, very well preserved and with lovely views and I also saw Iguanas fantastic animals, I wouldn't mind a couple in my garden.

Onwards then to Dominica, but so much for a favourable slant of the wind which had gone to the southeast. Then halfway across the wind died. I slopped about in the residual swell for what seemed like a decent interval then resorted to the motor. Anchoring in Prince Rupert Bay I noticed that Harvey and Rita's boat was here. I'd seen them last in Antigua, and later bumped into them ashore at the Blue Bay Bar. Barely ashore this, you land on a slightly wobbly wooden jetty and the waves lap at the front of the bar terrace, a nice spot.

Moving on to Roseau was a strange day wind wise, everything from flat calms to gentle sailing breezes and 25 knots and from all different directions. It made it difficult to get the sails right and I lost count of reefs in, reefs out, yankee furled away, yankee unfurled. Made for a frustrating day. Eventually I picked up one of Sea Cat's moorings once at Roseau. But the strange southwest swell that we had been having for the past few days made it anything but a restful night. I had planned to stay a while and visit the interior but in view of the swell I left early next morning. The forecast was for easterly 15 knot winds- which would have been lovely. Passing Scotts Head at the south of the island was gusty as might be expected but then it settled down to a steady southeast 18 knots. Well I could live with that even though it meant being close-hauled rather than on a more comfortable reach for the 26 miles across to Martinique. Later the wind dropped to average about 13 knots and a gentle sea state but after a hour or so of this the wind was up to 20 knots plus and the sea a bit more agitated and then 25 lots of wind and then later everything from 5 knots, virtual calms to 25 knots, difficult sailing. Eventually we were in the lee of

Martinique and no wind but a slop of a sea. Never mind not so far to St Pierre to anchor.

St Pierre was the site of a big volcanic disaster in 1902 when Mt Pele erupted, engulfing the town, at the time the biggest in Martinique, in a fireball of superheated gas. There were just 2 survivors, an estimated 29,933 people died and 12 ships at anchor in the bay were destroyed. Today many ruins remain, still blackened around the edges, the population is about 6,000. the town is quite interesting and Mt Pele quiet.

After a couple of days here it was on to Fort De France. A strong wind on the nose so tacking. It was May Day so everything was shut but the beach and park were humming with activity.

Another day I took a "taxi collective" (the equivalent of a bus) out through the busy outskirts and across the middle fertile agricultural parkland of the island past plantations of bananas and sugar cane fields to La Francoise, a quiet little town - not much there but it enabled me to see more of the island.

It was time to leave Fort de France, supplies bought, sail covers off, all made ready to hoist the anchor but the weather thought otherwise, blowing 25 knots in the anchorage and the bay a mass of white horses. No I thought I don't have to go, so I didn't.

The forecast was better for next day so dawn saw me hauling in the anchor. A nice sailing breeze across the bay and down the coast but thereafter if was 22 knots plus, mostly more like 25 knots for the rest of the day. 2 reefs in the main and just the staysail up. The wind kicked up quite a sea at times and at one point a wave joined me in the cockpit, breaking over my head. Still one advantage of Caribbean sailing is that the water is not cold and you soon dry off, albeit a little salty. I made it to the shelter of Marigot Bay, St Lucia and anchored outside the lagoon. A scenic spot this, I decided to stay over next day and explore on-shore.

Next stop was Soufriere, just 10 miles down the coast, a most beautiful coast I must say. Soufriere Bay is dominated by the Pitons, two wonderful volcanic peaks. I moored off the bat cave but it was a little rolly here so later moved across the bay hoping it would be quieter off the town.

Soufriere was the jumping off point for crossing to St Vincent. A dawn start saw me away, motoring as it was calm, across the bay and past the Pitons. Rounding Gros Piton point I had wind, gentle at first and could set a course for St Vincent. Later the wind strengthened a little, but a nice beam wind this and not too bad a sea and Sea Bear responded by showing 6 knots on the log, go Bear go, there were 40 miles to go so it was great to get good speed. I even saw some dolphins, the first I have seen in the Caribbean.

Much later as we neared the north end of St Vincent the wind picked up again, to be expected as it accelerates around the end of the island and the sea a little livelier so I put the first reef in the main. A bit later I felt the need for a 2nd reef in the main and to furl the yankee as it was getting a bit of a handful. However no sooner than I had done that, the wind dropped and then a calm. We were in the lee of the island, thereafter the wind was a little fitful but we slid calmly along the sea being flat in the lee and entered Wallilabou Bay. This was the main setting for the film "Pirates Of the Caribbean". A mooring buoy picked up and a stern line led to the old pilings with the aid of a boat boy and Sea Bear was snug. It had been a good fast passage. Time for a swim then later a beer ashore. I met and chatted with the lovely American couple off the catamaran moored next to me, Lew and Bev and we ate together, lovely grilled fish, Amberjack, I had never had his before, very tasty.

It was so peaceful and lovely here, I walked for about 4 hours the next day firstly up the valley then back to the beach. Here I watched some strange ritual involving 3 corpulent ladies, a man with a bell, a book and a bag of what I think were flower petals, much anointing with sea water, bathing, dunking and bell ringing. It went on for a long time and gave some amusement to a man who came down to bathe and who I chatted with. I continued the walk along through Keartons and to Barrouallie, the next village along the coast. All very scenic and interesting, I got the impression that they don't see many tourists or "whities", as some local youths called me, around these parts.

St Vincent is a pretty poor island, you can tell partly because the boat boys and fisherman have little rowing boats, not the big piroques with big outboard motors like other islands, some of the boat boys that sell fruit just paddle around on a surf board. The fisherman row 3 miles or so out to sea in these little boats to go fishing, its quite incredible. Ashore some of the tiny shacks that people live in too speak of poverty.

St Vincent was beautiful, I loved it there and to think I nearly passed it by because it has a bad reputation for boat boys and robberies from boats.

It was just a short hop to Bequia, part of the Grenadines. Sailing down the coast of St Vincent I had fickle winds but like the stubborn fool I am at times I persisted in sailing rather than resorting straightaway to the engine. Clearing the coast the wind freshened, it was time to shorten sail. I settled on staysail and double reefed main, quite enough with the wind at 22-24 knots and gusting higher. Admiralty Bay I am glad to say is big with plenty of room to anchor, I was glad of that in the conditions. I headed for what I thought might be the calmer part of the bay and as luck would have it anchored quite by chance next to Lew and Bev's catamaran.

In the night it really blew and rained too. I was glad of the rain as it washed all the salt spray off the boat, she had become a very salty Sea Bear.

With the salt washed off I took advantage next day to clean up the stainless of Martha which badly needed doing. It was still very windy and the sea choppy so I didn't bother blowing up the dinghy to go ashore, there was plenty to do aboard. In the evening Lew and Bev gave me a ride into town, the advantage of a big catamaran is being able to carry a bigger and hence drier tender. We had a few drinks, some food and listened to some guys playing guitars and singing, a very pleasant evening.

Other days I explored the town, which didn't take long as it was so small, and shopped at the market for fresh fruit and vegetables. I walked over to Industry via Spring estate. At Industry, strangely named, you couldn't imagine a more peaceful place, was a turtle sanctuary run by a delightful old guy. As a youth, in common with many islanders the had dug out the eggs and caught turtles to eat. But now he saw that had been wrong behaviour and he was a strong conservationist. It was nice to see turtles close up and he was doing a great job to help preserve this endangered species.

I left Bequia just after dawn, ran out of the bay and rounded Grand Cay. A wrecked freighter here reminds one of the potential dangers of sailing here. A lovely broad reach with moderate winds took us to Canouan which I passed by carrying on towards Mayreau passing between the Baleine rocks and Catholic Island with its shoals. The wind was picking up a little, time to furl the jib, only it wouldn't so a quick trip to the foredeck to haul it down and lash it to the deck. Then it was past the eastern side of Union Island, avoiding all the reefs of Palm Island and into the reef ringed harbour of Clifton. Forewarned that the holding was not good for anchoring I took a mooring buoy. It felt strange to be on the east side of an island facing the Atlantic with the ever present roar of surf on the reef, but the reef absorbed all the waves and it was calm inside. It had been a good passage, 30 miles in 6 hours. I went visit ashore to complete departure formalities as I was leaving the St Vincent Grenadines, the next island being Grenadian.

In the morning I walked up Fort hill above the town for some great views, although it was a little hazy towards the Tobago Keys. Back to the boat, time for a swim of course then off for the short sail to Carriacou in the afternoon.

After an uneventful passage I anchored off Hillsborough, there was only 1 other yacht here but there was a couple of Venezuelan fishing boats. These are very distinctive in style with a very high prow and a covered foredeck.

Ashore Hillsborough was very sleepy, it was a Sunday but formalities were soon completed at Customs in the police station. It seemed no buses run on a Sunday so I put off a visit to Windward until the next day. I wanted to visit Windward because they still build wooden boats in the traditional way on the beach there. A bus ride took me there next day and it was lovely to see this traditional craft still practised. Apparently they have quite a party when they launch them, it would be good to be there for that.

In the afternoon I moved around the corner to Tyrell Bay, this is the favoured anchorage for cruisers at Carriacou, so there were lots of yachts here.

At Tyrell Bay there is a mangrove lagoon or swamp which is a protected area for mangrove oysters so I took the dinghy there and rowed up it. Supposedly there are iguanas there but I didn't see any.

Last minute as ever I arranged for some boat storage in Trinidad. The first place I emailed an enquiry too said they were full, which put me in a mild panic, have I left it too late? what if they are all full? However the next two places I contacted said they had room so I reserved a lift out for 1st June, the official start of the hurricane season - I just had to get there now.

Dawn saw me away from Tyrell Bay to make the passage to Grenada. The direct course to the west coast of Grenada passes over a submerged volcano, Kick 'em Jenny, around which there is an exclusion zone, the size of which depends on the current level of activity. It was quiet at that moment. I thought I might pass to the east of the zone passing close to the island of Isle de Ronde and the rocks of the Sisters. There was however a strong current setting to the west and to counteract it I would need to be hard on the wind, so instead I choose to free off a little and pass Kick 'em Jenny to the west

I closed the Grenada coast near Gros Point and under its lee the seas were quieter and the wind lighter and more fickle. It looked a lovely island with forested mountains tumbling down to the sea. Eventually we arrived off St Georges at which point the wind picked up to 25 knots. Isn't it always the way, nice winds all day then coming up to anchor the wind decides to blast away! Just to make life interesting I guess. Anyway lots of room so I put the anchor down in 5 meters and lots of chain out so holding well.

No anchoring is allowed in the Lagoon at St George anymore, its been developed for a marina, and the Carenage is reserved for fishing boats so the anchorage is quite a dinghy ride out of the town but worthwhile for a look around. I overheard a guide giving a chat to a group of tourists. He was telling them a little about the American invasion of Grenada in 1983. An invasion which was both illegal under international law and widely condemned although not unfortunately by Mrs Thatchers government, who publicly supported it. The guide said that of all the things that the Americans could have done post invasion to help the country like schools and hospitals instead they gave them Kentucky fried chicken and coca cola.

A few days here and I moved on to Prickly Bay just a few miles around the corner. This is the favoured anchorage for cruising folk. Here I had a chance encounter with another Vancouver, this a 32 "Naomi" with Ian who had recently completed a solo circumnavigation over 4 years. I had tea with him and a good gam. He too was on his way to Trinidad to store the boat for the hurricane season.

It is 80 miles from the south coast of Grenada to the north coast of Trinidad, too far for a daylight passage, so an afternoon or evening departure was the way to go, but what time exactly? Leave too early and with a fast passage it would still be dark on closing the Trinidad coast, something to be avoided. Leave too late and with a slow passage the risk of arriving as evening falls the following day. So a noon departure was fixed on, the forecast looked good and leaving Wednesday should ensure an arrival before the weekend so we wouldn't have to pay overtime to customs and immigration. Ian decided to leave at the same time.

Raising the anchor I headed out to sea, taking care to give a good clearance to some offshore rocks, the Porpoises, sometimes hard to see but identified by the breaking waves over them. Once past these I could set a course, allowing for the west flowing current. It soon became apparent that the current was strong so I had to adjust the course to windward, not the nice beam reach I was hoping for but a close reach about 60 degrees off the wind, which was nice and steady at 15 to 17 knots and the sea state was kind. Time to settle back and enjoy the passage, Martha seeing to the steering I just had to monitor progress and watch for shipping. Indeed about 3 hours out 2 ships appeared, one in front and one behind. In the event one passed safely across my bows about a mile off and the other overtook me on my port side about a mile off.

Sunset and although it was cloudy, the moon, about three quarters full, shone through them so the night was not dark and it was a pleasant sail.

There are a couple of gas platforms about 25 mile north off the Trinidad coast and they provide a good seamark, lit up like Christmas trees they can be seen miles off. Dawn saw us about 10 miles off the coast but gradually the wind was dropping, a little later I spied a sail and then the AIS beeped, it was Ian in "Naomi". With him being a bigger and faster boat I was very surprised to see him again and be so close after such a long passage. It transpired he had been worried by the set of the current and gone a good way to windward to avoid being set to the West whereas I had sailed a slighter shorter course.

Calm fell so we motored the last miles, closing the Boca de Monos, a passage between the mainland and Monos island. The coast was very dramatic, steep wooded cliffs falling to the sea and there were hundreds of pelicans flying in formation. Once through the channel we turned into Chaguaramas bay, threading a way through all the boats large and small. We tied up alongside the customs dock to report our arrival. 80 miles plus, the log had stopped working awhile probably blocked by seaweed, there has been a lot of pelagic Sargasso weed this year. Ian had logged 100 miles.

Chaguaramas was where I had decided to haul the boat out and lay her up for the hurricane season. It is a busy commercial shipping area but ashore there are several boatyards with very good layup and work facilities, everything from sailmakers to steel fabricators and several chandleries. A couple of days were spent on a mooring buoy in the bay, a bit rock and roll at times because of all the wake from passing boats but then it was lift out time. First I wanted to fill with diesel, a full tank limits condensation forming in the tank leading to water in the fuel. 7.30 Monday morning though there were two fishing boats alongside the fuel jetty and they didn't look like they would be moving soon. There was room inshore but space was tight, I thought I could get in OK but could I get out again? Hell lets try! I manoeuvred in OK, got tied up and filled with diesel. Getting out was even tighter than it had looked at first, well it had to be done, crunch time you might say only I managed to avoid the crunch and turn around unscathed with inches to spare. Next stop the lift out dock where the yard hands were ready to take my lines and soon Sea Bear was hoisted from the water and on stands in the yard. It felt very strange to be on the boat and it was not moving.

The next few days were spent laying up - hosing the boat down to wash all the salt off, stripping off sails and rigging and washing them, general cleaning, polishing the stainless work. I did take a day off to take the bus to Port of Spain for a look around. I visited the botanical gardens etc. but that was the limit of exploring Trinidad before catching a plane back to UK. There would be plenty of time to explore later when I returned to the boat later in the year. So it was back to the UK for a few months, to enjoy the English summer? and catch up with family and friends.

Sea Bear In Victoria dock

Caleto de Sebo, Gracioso

Kasbah des Oudayas, Maroc

Crossing the Atlantic

Wendy at the helm in Antigua

English Harbour

Fishing boat, Ille a Vache

Portebelo, Panama

Baie Hanavae, Fatu Hiva

Teehapoa, Tahiti

Bora Bora

School visit, Tonga

12. Up through the Windwards and Leewards

"A ship in a harbor is safe, but that's not what ships are built for."
(William Shedd)

After a summer in the UK I returned to Trinidad in early September. My first task was to make a list of jobs to be done. Back in the UK boat maintenance, was always a cold affair, bundled up in many layers to try and keep warm in a boatyard on the edge of the Menai Straits with a cold northeasterly wind blowing.

The novelty here was that it was hot, almost too hot, but so much easier to tackle washing the boat down clad in just shorts and a pleasure to turn the hosepipe on oneself. Painting and varnishing was much easier, no worrying about minimum temperatures. After re-painting the red sheer band and polishing the topsides, Sea Bear was looking OK for a 29 year old lady. There was still plenty to do mind, things to fix, things to overhaul which kept me busy.

It was not all work no play. My favourite place for lunch was the roti shack in the boat yard, queuing you could watch iguanas in the trees and butterflys as big as your hand with flashes of incandescent blue, flitting about. Mmm the rotis were good too.

I now had a folding bike so I had some nice rides. Through the forest to Morne Catherine at 540m - well actually it was hard uphill work, a multitude of different types of trees and vegetation and lots of noisy birds and insects, with plenty of butterflies. A glorious freewheel downhill for 6 miles led back to the coast.

Another day along the Tucker valley to Macqueripe Bay on the north coast. Here I swam along with plenty of pelicans who were fishing unconcernedly amongst all the bathers - quite an incredible experience.

On another ride I took in what they called the bamboo cathedral, beautiful stands of bamboo arching gracefully over the track. Here I also saw the monkeys for which the area is renowned.

In the evenings I sometimes went for a beer in the Wheelhouse bar by the Tropical Marine boatyard. Here I had the choice of Carib - real beer is Carib or Stag - real men drink Stag. I swopped between the two to cover all eventualities. One evening a week the bar set up a barbecue and laid on a set dinner which was fantastic value and very tasty food - barbecued swordfish with cauliflower cheese plus vegetables and salad. The portions were so generous that they served it to you on two plates. This event was always well attended by a mixture of cruisers and locals so was a very social evening.

Eventually after all the work, Sea Bear was back in the water berthed in the little creek around the side of the yard. I got the rigger to check over and adjust the standing rigging.

December and hurricane season was over, it was time to resuming cruising. Immigration and customs were visited, provisions and duty free gin and rum purchased, it was time to cast off the lines, reverse out of the dock, motor through all the moored boats in Chaguaramas Bay and then through the Boca passage to the open sea. It was a bit windier and the sea a little rougher than I would have liked for a first passage after such a long lay off but you just have to deal with what the weather gods send you. It turned out to be a long hard passage, hard on the wind the whole way. 22 hours later I sailed into Prickly Bay Grenada and anchored. No rest yet though, the dinghy to inflate and customs and immigration to visit then a hot walk to the bank for funds. Later Martin and Martha, a Dutch couple I had met in Trinidad came by and took me to happy hour and half price pizza at the bar. So fed and watered I could retire to my bunk 36 hours after last lying down.

To explore the area I bused up into the mountains, visited the Grand Etang lake and walked in the forest, it was cool up here and there were some nice views.

Ged, my son arrived from the UK. We visited St Georges and the Grand Anse, a very lovely beach. Here we ate some jerk chicken barbecued on the beach and whilst waiting for it to be cooked we had a beer or two. "Soon come man" has a whole different meaning here in the laid back Caribbean. The chef wouldn't hurry the barbecuing process, he knew what he was doing and the wait was well justified by the end result, chicken that was juicy and tender with that distinctive jerk flavour. Another day we went to a dinghy concert, the band played from a raft moored in Phare Bleau bay, we were on an adjacent raft and lots of cruisers turned up in their dinghies. The music and atmosphere was good.

Leaving Prickly Bay we made a short hop to Dragon Bay and had time for a spot of snorkelling before our sundowners.

First light next day we were underway, up the coast then past Kick 'em Jenny and Diamond rock to Tyrell Bay Carriacou. Ashore later we had a very nice fish dinner in the Slipway restaurant, fresh Tuna for me and Mai Mai for Ged. The following day we visited the mangrove lagoon then a walk to and along Paradise beach finishing with drinking rum with the locals at Banana Joe's, a very laid back character.

Moving on we moored off Sandy island, this just a strip of coral and sand with a few palm trees. It was very windy so the snorkelling was not so good as it could have been. On then to Hillsborough, a bus over to Windward to look at the boat building and a walk towards the north of the island.

Next stop was Petite Martinique, a more laid back island would I think be hard to find in the Caribbean. No other yachts here, no tourists.

On to Union island, we bought fresh tuna steaks from a fisherman and walked up Fort hill for the views towards our next objective the uninhabited Tobago Cays. Careful navigation is needed to visit these surrounded as they are by reefs but they are a fabulous place to visit. We swam, saw iguanas ashore and treated ourselves to barbecued lobster.

Still strong winds for our passage to Bequia, 25 to 30 knots with a lively sea. Leeway, wind, waves, current all pushing us westward so it was hard work to gain the easting we needed.

We discovered the hard way that the holding in Admiralty bay was not great, the bottom being sand and rubble, when we were awoken at 3.30 am by the anchor alarm. Not much fun that time in the morning re-anchoring. Later for peace of mind we took a mooring buoy.

Christmas day was spent here, we had lunch on the terrace of a restaurant overlooking the bay followed by a walk along the beach, went swimming and rounded off the day with rum punch at a Rasta spot.

Another rough but thankfully short passage took us to St Vincent. In the lee of the island all was much calmer and we arrived at Cumberland Bay to anchor with Joseph the Rastaman taking a stern line ashore tied to a tree on the beach.

A walk ashore confirmed the friendliness of the locals with greetings and chats. One love man.

We both wanted to stay longer here in St Vincent but Ged's plane from Martinique would not wait. We cleared out from Chateaubelair further up the coast, a desperately poor place this but the locals super friendly and helpful.

By the time we arrived in St Lucia we were very salty from spray and motoring the last miles into Soufriere was a race against the dark. Sometimes you can be very thankful that there are boat boys and they helped us to a vacant mooring buoy. Anchoring is not allowed here as it is a Marine park. One good thing about this passage was the catching of a small tuna by our trolled line, it provided a tasty evening meal.

A pleasant sail on flat water took us to Rodney Bay. Its the sort of place I normally avoid, a big marina with condominiums, holiday resorts etc. but an ideal jumping off spot for crossing to Martinique.

Martinique is north from St Lucia so at least we did not have to fight to make easting. With calmer seas and a beam wind we flew along surprising both of us by our speed and the ease of it. So we arrived by midday to anchor in Grande Anse d'Arlet. Jean Mitchell who I had first meet in Northern Spain over a year ago was here and spotting Sea Bear rowed over to invite us for t-punch. There are lots of turtles here so Ged eventually got to swim with a turtle when snorkelling.

We went to a Creole restaurant on the beach for lunch before the short hop to Fort de France. Ashore there was a lot going on, music, bands, loads of people. We had to keep checking we were not a day out and it wasn't New Years Eve already. Back on the boat there seemed more boats at anchor and lots of motorboats arriving in the dark, it was a bit chaotic but a police boat patrolling in front of us stopped boats passing beyond us. The reason was a grand firework display from the fort and on our boat we had front row seats as it were. I told Ged it was arranged specially for a grand send off for him.

In the morning it was time for Ged to catch the bus to the airport to fly home.

With Ged departed I made my way back to Grande Anse for a relaxing couple of days before feeling the need to move on. A day sail then took me to St Pierre for an overnight anchorage before the passage to Dominica. I decided not to stop in Dominica this time as the weather was a little unsettled and very rainy. I just had a couple of overnights anchorage at Rosseau and Portsmouth.

On then to Guadeloupe, by passing Les Saintes this time as I had visited them twice before I headed for Pointe de Pitre. A quiet anchorage here but not the most scenic in the Caribbean with container docks and the like. Still it was handy for the laundry and to stock up on supplies from the supermarket. It being a French island of course that meant cheap French wine and cheese.

On then to Saint Francois out to the east of the long thin peninsular that sticks out to the Atlantic. Endless tacking that day but the wind was light and the seas flat. For that I was grateful, for the entrance to St Francois is through a narrow passage in the reefs, fortunately well buoyed but with breaking waves both sides. Anchoring in the lagoon was very peaceful. I hitched hiked to Point les Chateaux next morning. This is a spectacular point and I walked along the coast. I found myself on a nudist beach so not having taken swimming things with me I availed myself of the opportunity for a skinny dip. Further on past Pt des Gourdes a welcome beer in a bar refreshed me before hitching back.

Marie-Galante was my next stop, I had to motor as the winds had deserted me but it wasn't too far. I anchored in St Louis Bay, a wonderful wide shallow bay with water so crystal clear. Marie-Galante is the island that time forget. Bullock carts were used to take the rum from the distillery down to the beach and the barrels then put on a raft to take out to a two masted barque at anchor in the bay. I walked around the headland to Anse Canot, just another lovely Caribbean beach.

For the passage back to the main island of Guadeloupe the wind was light so I rigged the big red and white cruising chute. It got a bit of a handful when the wind piped up later and I handed it just short of rounding Pt a Launay at the southern tip of Guadeloupe. In the lee it was flat calm so I motored to Riverie Sens, where I anchored off a black sand beach. The holding here was none too good, it being very weedy, so I moved on to a vacant mooring buoy.

Next morning a walk took me to Basse Terre, a bus to St Caude and then I hitched up to the car park at the start of the track up the Soufriere volcano. At first this led through rain forest then emerged onto drier savanne before tackling the final ascent of the cone. It was a little bit misty on the top so the fine views were missing but the craters, vents and fumoroles were impressive with a fine sulphurous smell, well worth the effort of ascent.

Next day it was on to Deshaises at the north of the island. Ashore time to search out Madame Sorbet with her delicious coconut flavoured sorbet. A long queue to complete departure formalities then a beer on a terrace overlooking the bay. Back at the boat it was time to deflate and stow the dinghy for an early start in the morning to make for Antigua.

I had a reasonable crossing to Antigua although the wind was very variable so lots of sail configuration changes. I arrived in Freeman's bay English Harbour and spotted Harvey and Rita's yacht so said hello before finding a spot to anchor. They invited me to dinner and drinks which was very nice.

Highlights of the next few days were a beach barbecue, a walk up Shirley Heights with Rita and Harvey. A walk over Middle Ground to swim at Pigeon Beach, a cycle ride to Bethesda (I lived in Bethesda North Wales for a long time so just had to visit its twin), the donkey sanctuary there was a bonus. I was invited to a tot and toast at the Naval tot club followed by fish Friday. I had a long bike ride to Carlisle Bay down and back up Fig Tree Drive, this was a bit of a beast of a hill in parts and hilly the rest of way too, the legs were pretty tired after this little excursion.

It had been unsettled and squally for a few days but when the winds eased and the seas were calmer, I made for Green Island and then into Nonsuch Bay. This was through the reefs, eyeball navigation this, for which the sun very unhelpfully hid behind a cloud, you need good light to see the reefs, but through OK and anchored in Ayres Creek, I just had to go there didn't I? Very little there, very quiet, I was the only boat there.

When leaving Nonsuch bay there was quite a swell on York Bank built up by the strong winds, so not much fun but Sea Bear coped well as usual. Then a fast run just under yankee, rolly and with breaking waves past English Harbour, through the Goats Head channel between Cadie's reef and the mainland past Pelican Island and into the lee of the west coast to anchor off Jolly Harbour.

A 45 mile crossing took me to the island of Nevis. Closing the coast at the southern tip, Dogwood point it was easy to misjudge how far off you were. At first I thought I was a mile offshore but realised what I thought were trees were just bushes and I closer inshore than I thought and the depth shallow. Easily corrected by a slight course change but a reminder to be ever vigilante. At least one yacht (another Vancouver no less) had been wrecked here. I picked up a mooring buoy off Pinney's Beach.

It is a lovely spot to just chill out and relax, a beautiful long beach, clear waters and some nice beach bars. One is owned by Mark Roberts a Vancouver owner, so it was good to pay him a visit again, have a beer or two and catch up on things.

There was a beautiful modern classic 56' sloop moored near by, "Spirited Lady of Fowey", the skipper, Susie, dropped by one morning. Mark had mentioned that I was thinking of going to Cuba and that was her intention too. I was invited to her boat for a meal and we swopped notes. It was truly a lovely boat but must be a bit high maintenance with acres of teak decks and varnished woodwork.

Next day she took me to the hot springs, the existence of which I was unaware. The water was very hot, just bearable but on getting out you felt a little chilly in contrast although the air temperature was in the thirties, a strange feeling.

One day I watched for ages a big shoal of little fish no more than about an inch swim about the boat, all changing direction at once just like you might see on a nature programme on the telly then some bigger fish perhaps 8 to 18 inches dart in so quick to grab a mouthful of them.

I cycled around the island, the opposite direction to last year and enjoyed it, legs a bit tired afterwards - they don't get enough use!

It would've been easy to stay here for ages but I felt the need to move on again, it was a long way to Cuba from here and first I wanted to go to St Maarten to stock up and then I'd a mind to call in at the British Virgin Islands.

It was 3 am when I slipped the mooring at Pinney's beach, up past St Kitts then Statia and across to St Maarten, anchoring in Simpson Bay after a passage of 15 hrs for the 61n miles. I cleared in the next morning and when the bridge opened I moved into the lagoon.

I liked the bar Lagoonies, set on the edge of the lagoon with its own dinghy dock, a lively place often with live music, happy hour here and a bottle of Presidente beer is just 1 US$.

The island being duty free, booze is amazingly cheap so I stocked up, Rum at 5 US $ a bottle a bargain and since I am bound for ex pirate islands next we needs some rum aarh!

Stocked up too on provisions so two big supermarket shops, one on the Dutch side and another on the French side, staggering back each time with a full rucsac and two laden shopping bags, that should provide me with the staples for a couple of months or more.

The other thing the island is good for is chandleries, a big Budget Marine and big Island Water World, so I was able to get some necessaries including a pilot book and some charts of Cuba.

A few little jobs on the boat done and I was ready to move on again before I became a permanent fixture propping up a bar stool at Lagoonies!

13. To the British Virgin Islands and Dominican Republic

"The charm of single handed sailing is not solitude, but independence."
(Claud Worth)

A false start - The forecast was OK but I didn't get very far. Firstly there was a hold up at the lifting bridge. A big motor boat, a superyacht went through oh so slowly, it must have taken him 15 minutes or so. The bridge keeper was getting really irate with him over the vhf, telling him he was causing a holdup and that he must clear the channel now, quite amusing, the keeper obviously cared nothing, no deference shown for the megarich man in his superyacht, who I bet not often gets talked to like that.

Anyway I got through eventually but then along came the first of many squalls, you couldn't see them coming as they came over the mountain so little warning, high winds and torrential rain, and visibility down to about nothing. After about the third or fourth in about an hour I decided to go back. I was drenched and fed up with it. Two more on the way back including one just as I was about the drop the anchor. It was thoroughly unpleasant.

Anyway I made the right decision because the rest of day, evening and night was not nice weatherwise at all.

The afternoon of the next day was a bit of a repeat performance, a really nasty squall about half an hour after I'd left. Martha the self steering, couldn't cope and the boat rounded up and made a dash for the shore so I fought that and steered offshore. With the full yankee out I had way too much sail up for 30 knots of wind I then struggled to roll up the yankee, lost a sheet to the wind, normally the stopper knot stops it pulling through the blocks but not this time. Anyway I got the sail furled and just lay ahull for a while until the squall passed, then I could sort it all out. Fortunately just the one squall this time thereafter the weather looked fine. It was a bit windy mind, 25 knots or so but downwind sailing, it was a bit rolly with a sizeable swell. After sunset I had a nice half moon until it set about 4am. By dawn we had done 75 miles and I could see the island of Virgin Gorda, perfect timing. Switching on the GPS to double check and were 6 miles from our waypoint at the end of Virgin Gorda and bang on target, pleasing dead reckoning that. Past Pajaros Point we just had to thread a way past the reefs and Richard Branson's private island (Necker Island) and past Pull or be Dammed Point and so into Gorda Sound.

I cleared in at Gun Creek, a quick and painless process and then moved over to anchor off Prickly Pear island on the other side of the sound. A lovely spot this, although the beach restaurant was closed, dashing my hopes of some nice food. I thought I would go there for lunch the next day but in the meantime a cruise ship had arrived and anchored off and they had taken over the place, so hopes were dashed again. I moved over to Leverick bay and lunched here.

Next morning I took a walk, hoping to get up to the top of Virgin Gorda peak, I got close but a number of tracks I tried turned out to be dead ends and I had no map, so in the end contented myself with a stunning viewpoint overlooking the whole of the North Sound.

I moved on to St Thomas, the main town of Virgin Gorda intending to visit the Baths, a spectacular mooring with white sand beaches and huge granite boulders. This is a very popular spot so apparently all the moorings get taken by mid morning. It was beautiful calm evening but things changed in the night, a brisk northeasterly arrived and with it a big swell, it caused a few boats to drag and they had to move in the middle of the night.

Next day was no day for the Baths so I had a boisterous sail across to Tortola and found shelter in Fat Hogs Bay, it was still blowing 25 knots but there was flat water in the shelter behind the reef. Ashore in the evening I dined in a local eatery with a barbecue set up outside, jerk chicken, delicious.

The wind had departed in the morning so I returned to the Baths, the swell was still running crashing into the boulders so there was no chance to go ashore but I took a mooring and had lunch before returning to Fat Hogs Bay.

Next stop on Tortola was Road Town, the Capital, but I didn't stay long, about an hour, a soulless place I found it, all new concrete buildings and a busy road. Instead a nice sail across Drake Passage, past Pelican Island and the Indians took me to the Bight on Norman Island. A proper old pirate haunt this and reputably the setting for the book, Treasure Island. Ashore I dined in the Pirates Bight restaurant on barbecued ribs. A walk ashore in the morning took me to the highest point of the island with lovely views.

On then to Sopers hole and passing through Thatch Island Cut across to the island of Joss Van Dyke. It was as I'd feared a bit choppy in the bay here, with too much south in the wind so I returned to Sopers Hole. Here I ran into Richard and Eilish again in their lovely homebuilt steel gaff cutter "Granuaile". I had first met them in Northern Spain.

I decided it was time to leave the BVI, it is undoubtedly a beautiful place and would be a perfect cruising ground if only it weren't such a perfect cruising ground and hence so crowded out with charter boats. Its expensive too, the tourist and charter boats push up the prices and its the most expensive place I have been in the Caribbean so far.

I spent my last day in BVI at Sopers Hole, checking over the boat and getting some supplies. Someone once said that cruising is about fixing your boat in exotic locations and there is truth in this. I overhauled the bilge pump as I discovered it to be leaking at the flange and dripping salt water over the engine, not good. A new diaphragm dug out of the boson's stores aboard was fitted to cure this.

I slipped the mooring early to run down the Narrows between Tortola and St Johns, part of the American Virgins. I could then turn towards the Windward Passage, so with the wind more on the beam up went the reefed mainsail and I passed through the Durloe Cays. Later passing between Cruz bay and Steven Cay I carefully avoided Skipper Jacob's Rock, a more wicked looking rock I have rarely seen, sharp and pointed and I wondered on the unfortunate skipper who it was named after. The last obstacle in threading my way through the islands was the Dog rocks and then I could set a course to pass south of the Spanish Virgin Islands, south of Costa Rica and Mona Island before arriving at Boca Chica in the Dominican Republic. It was a slow passage of 300 miles due to light winds and calms, but a fairly stress free one so I was happy to settle for that. On the evening of the fourth day out I motored through the buoyed channel leading through the reef and behind a small island and into Marina Zar Par. I was soon tied up alongside to be greeted by a welcoming committee of the marina manager, the coast guard and M2, the drug enforcement agency. After a cursory search of the boat all was OK, it being Sunday Immigration could wait until the morning.

If you wanted one word to describe the Dominican Republic it would be loud! Music is played everywhere at full volume, even little general shops have a speaker the size of a fridge balanced on the counter cranked up to full volume. Its a lively place to be sure, a crazy place, music, teaching salsa dancing in the courtyard of a hairdressing saloon, a couple dancing on the shop floor of an off-licence, bars with people outside filling the pavement. Music here is more Latin American - salsa music.

I visited Santa Domingo by bus. I wandered around the old colonial district, very quiet and peaceful tidy and clean, some lovely buildings and streets, and I found the statue to Christopher Columbus. The rest of the city is mad by contrast, traffic with seemingly no rules, street sellers, street stalls noisy and busy and chaotic. I had some lovely pineapple - the fruit and veg here is about the best I have seen in the Caribbean and the cheapest.

The marina was situated on the edge of the town of Boca Chica which is a very popular and busy holiday resort and beach. You could walk along a track by the beach to the main part of the town past many food and drink shacks. It was perfectly safe to do this in the daytime but apparently unsafe at night. The Norwegian lads were about to walk back this way late one evening but the police stopped them and advised them to go via the road. Asking why prompted the policeman to pull out his pistol, point it at the lads and ask what will you do if a robbers does this to you? The point was taken.

After a few days I was ready to leave but the weather forecast was for very strong winds of 35/40 knots so I stayed.

I spent an evening sitting on a crate on the pavement outside a store drinking cheap rose wine from an ice filled plastic cup with the manager from the marina. He had asked me if I wanted to join him and visit his home and he took me on the back of his little motorbike to his house down a muddy yard, the living space was tiny. We walked through streets and alleys to the store where wine was bought and we sat and talked. He said that they live like rabbits, the street are pretty crowded, most life is lived outside it seems, cheek by jowl as it were. He seem to be at work from 8 till 6 and only gets 1 day off a week, it must be a pretty tough life. Later he ran me back on his bike, it was getting dark, no lights, no crash hats and in flip flops. The roads are potholed and with open drains across them. I felt a bit privileged to get some insight into life here.

Eventually the winds eased and I made an overnight passage to Salinas. A lovely bay where they have extensive salt pans to get sea salt. Shortly after I arrived I had 30 knots of wind and suffered a dragging anchor, the holding wasn't so good so I had an anxious and unpleasant time for a while. After a day or so I moved just around the corner to Palmars de Ocoa, just another lovely beach with a little fishing town backed by mountains. On then across the bay to Santa Cruz de Barahona, quite a busy town, a sheltered anchorage but not so scenic. I had thought I might stay here, perhaps visit the mountains and a big lake inland where they have crocodiles but the only place to leave a dinghy seemed to be a rough concrete wharf and there was a bad surge there so I decided to move on. Perhaps I was getting fed up of the Dominican Republic, or least the officialdom. To go from port to port you need a dispatchio from the coast guard and although officially they should be free, the officials ask for 20$, a bribe basically. Here they made a bit of a fuss but I just stonewalled them, said I had no dollars and eventually although they were not happy to say the least, they gave me a dispatchio and exit stamped my passport.

It was about 40 miles down the coast towards Capo Beata, where I took Canal de Beata between the Ilas Beata and the mainland. As soon as I gybed towards the passage the boat accelerated, there must have been quite a current running through here and the swell which had been troubling me all day disappeared and the depth dropped to around 4.5 to 5 metres. It was dark before I passed Cabo Falso so I could not stop at the Bay of Eagles, which would have been my last anchorage in Dominican Republic, instead I carried on another 150 miles past the coast of Haiti towards Il a' Vache, a satellite island some 6 miles off the coast of Haiti.

14. Hiati and Cuba.

*"I wanted freedom, open air, adventure. I found it on the sea." (Alain
Gerbaul)*

Spotting the light on Il a' Vache still some 8 miles away I hove to for a while so I would not arrive before the dawn.

Later running up between the island and the mainland I caught sight of the first of many of the traditional sailing fishing boats of the area and the first of the dugout canoes that they still use. Turning in to Baie Feret I had a welcoming committee of boat boys in dugout canoes all offering their services.

Here already at anchor where the young Norwegians, Olaf and Knut in their boat and Rene (French) and Rod (SA) who had left Boca Chica a few days before me. Hearing their tales made me glad that I had waited for the strong winds to pass. The Norwegians had suffered a knock down with their mast in the water in big rough seas, smashing their autopilot and solar panel, and bending the pushpit and some stanchions whilst the French boat had suffered damage to a sail, their gooseneck fitting and had lost a dinghy.

I took a ride over to the town Les Cayes on the mainland in one of the outboard powered local boats. This was mainly to visit a bank to get some Hiatian money, gourdes. I was a bit naughty in that I decided not to check into Haiti officially. Haiti is one of the poorest countries in the world and also reckoned to the most corrupt. I thought it best to avoid any dealings with officialdom.

At Les Cayes I did come across a simple commemorative plaque to the devastating earthquake of 2010, in this it is estimated that between 46,000 and 85,000 persons died and 1.6 million made homeless. That the figure is not known with certainty highlights the chaotic nature of Haiti.

Haiti has an interesting history, in 1791 there was a full blown slave revolt led by the black general Toussaint Louverture and shortly afterwards slavery was abolished in Hiati. France tried to reassert control but they were defeated and in 1804 Hiati declared itself as independent. However over the years Haiti has always been plagued by instability and oft times bloody conflict, there have been 32 coups.

Il a' Vache is a beautiful place, around the shores of the bay is a simple village Cai Coch, they have no electricity and no running water, although now they do have a few solar powered lights. There are no roads, no cars, some little motorbikes only. The people walk mostly, sometimes ride horses to get about and live by plot farming and fishing from wooden sailing boats or dugout canoes.

Ferret bay where I was anchored was once the haunt of the pirate Captain Henry Morgan who once in a spell of drunken revelry managed to blow up his own boat. The wreck is believed to have been discovered in 2004 by some researchers.

One day I walked over to the market at the village of Madame Bertram, pigs, goats, chickens, fish, vegetables, soap, rice all for sale spread out in chaotic fashion on rickety stalls amongst the mud and the garbage with sailing boats that have bought in the goods in the bay and women arriving with baskets of sweet potatoes or coconuts or breadfruit balanced on their heads to sell. It was a scene that could have been from hundreds of years ago.

Leaving Ile a' Vache and rounding Point l' Abacou I could set my course to run parallel to the coast. There certainly are some big mountains in Haiti so the scenery was quite spectacular. Another slow passage of 225 miles due to light winds but eventually I entered the channel leading to Santiago de Cuba and anchored off the marina at Punta Gorda just before sunset.

In the morning I dinghied to the dock to pick up the doctor and took her back to the boat. She asked me a few questions and took my temperature and pronounced me disease free. They take their health seriously and want to keep Cuba healthy. Then I visited the coast guard and answered their questions, there were no forms to fill in it being all on computer these days. They then inspected the boat, content with letting their sniffer dog, a cute little docile spaniel, have a good snuffle around. Then clearance and visa was issued and I was in Cuba.

I was offered a lift into Santiago, here I got some convertible pesos or cucs and then had a wander around, getting a bit lost but not too badly. It is a big sprawling city but first impression very clean, none of the litter and garbage strewn about that you see in the Dominican Republic. Old American cars a plenty, MZ motorbikes which brought back memories of my time as a motorcycle mechanic, horse drawn carts, big trucks which acted as buses. I bought a few vegetables at a farmers market and eventually took a taxi back.

I spent a few days anchored at Punta Gorda, I discovered the best way to get into Santiago was to take the ferry. I enjoyed wandering around to see the sights and listen to the music. The main square was Parque Cesapades and there were almost always a group of musicians playing there - think Buena Vista Social club.

There were also a couple of venues where you could wander into, sit down and listen to the music for a while. The main shopping street was wide pedestrian only and led up to another big square Plaza Delores, here were more musicians plus restaurants and bars.

There were two currencies in use here, the cuc which was worth a US dollar and is what as a tourist or foreigner you get given at the bank and the Cuban peso which is what the locals get paid in and use. I soon discovered that it was useful to have both and I changed some cuc to pesos, about 24 or 25 pesos to 1 cuc. It seemed better when buying vegetables or bread for instance to use pesos and some traders seemed reluctant to accept cuc. I also discovered Paladars, generally a few tables in someones front room right next to the kitchen where you could get Cuban homestyle cooking. Used by the locals and great value.

I cycled out to Castillo del Morro, a fortress built in 1600's to defend the entrance to the bay in which Santiago is built. It is well preserved and a world heritage site, well worth a look around and offered lovely views of the bay. I called in at a little beach, popular with the locals for a swim. I also went for a walk to a prominent limestone bluff inland by tiny paths through the bush and on top buzzards soaring just feet above my head.

The Norwegians lads, had arrived too, but they were off eastwards and northwards. I was still westward bound.

Next stop after leaving Santiago was Chivorico, here a tight entry between the reefs into a lovely little lagoon. Here I watched a man fishing from an inflated truck inner tube, common practise where few can afford a boat. On again to Marea del Portillo and an easier entry into a big lagoon this. On my first evening there and a 30 plus knot northerly arrived as dark fell, the anchor dragged so I put out the Bruce as a second anchor. In the midst of this the Guarda arrived in a little rowing boat, they were having quite a struggle in the wind and I was surprised to see them on a night like this. Ashore was a little fishing village, this was rural untouched Cuba, lovely. I got some peppers, tomatoes and cucumbers from a plot farmer, he wanted some fishhooks so I gave him some.

A short hop took me to Ensenada Tiburcio, I didn't like this entry, it started off easily enough, well marked with buoys but thereafter it was unmarked between a shoaling shore and unmarked reefs.

My next stop was the anchorage at Cabo Cruz, reached around a long breaking reef but at least well marked. The anchorage is some way from the town and the lighthouse and meant a long dinghy ride in, but it was worth a visit.

The next stretch westwards along the coast was the Gulf of Guacanayabo and Gulf of Anna Maria and the Jardines de la Reina. This is a labyrinth of hundreds of uninhabited cays, reefs and shoals. There are just a few fishermen but otherwise I was to be on my own, few cruisers come this way, it is wilderness unspoilt. The pilot guide recommends a good bow watch to look out for shoals and coral, being on my own meant I would have to do without, this led to a degree of apprehension about this stage.

To the next anchorage was too far to make in daylight so I left just before dark aiming to arrive at the entrance to the Canal de Cabenza del Este, which leads into the inshore passage behind the reefs by daylight. Here I would enter into the gulf of Guacanayabo.

It turned out to be a wild night, the wind got up and barely dropped below 30 knots all night, I was down to the third reef in the main and a reef in the staysail and of course I arrived at my waypoint for the canal whilst still dark so I decided to hove to for a while till dawn. With the wind out of the northeast passing through the canal, bashing into a nasty short chop was unpleasant but finally I arrived at Cayo Granada to drop the hook.

The following days I transited the Canal de Rancho Vieja and Canal del Pingue leading into the gulf of Anna Maria. The word canal gives the wrong impression, here it is used to denote a passage through the reefs. There are no banks, you are sailing through what looks like open waters with the occasional reef and cay visible and some few marker posts to guide you, but stray off track and you will be aground on the shoals! A series of anchorages at Cayo Chocolate, Cayo Manual Gomez, Cayo Ingles, Cayo Breton, Cayo Macho de Afuera and finally arriving at Casilda. In all this time I only saw 2 Cuban fishing boats. It had been a very intense experience, the peace, the silence were outstanding at times but it had been hard work, concentration being needed at all times.

Casilda is the nearest port to the town of Trinidad, this is a lovely historic city, one of the oldest in the New World founded in 1514 and is one of UNESCO's World Heritage sites. Well worth a visit and I spent a couple of days wandering around its cobbled streets.

On then to Cienfeugos about 35 miles down the coast. Here there is a fairly narrow entrance to a big enclosed bay and you anchor off the marina. A walk down the Malecon takes you into the busy city. There are some fine old colonial buildings and a nice plaza and I soon discovered my favourite bar where you could sit outside in the shade under a colonnade, drink beer and watch the world go by.

One day I took the bike and headed out into the country past vast orchards of mangos then just wild country side. After about 16 miles I ended up at Playa Blanca, a nice little beach so swam before heading back. I saw a real vaquero, complete with leather chaps and lariat as well as lots of horse drawn traps and of course old american cars.

All too soon my time was up, the month had flown by, my Cuban visa had run out, although I was tempted to renew it, it was time to leave and move on. Next stop the Cayman Islands 145 miles away.

15. Sister Islands Caves and Dragons and Jamaica

"On the ocean I never feel lonely. There's too much beauty - the sea, the wind, the sky, the animals and fish." (Tania Aebi)

Leaving Cienfeugos the big danger to avoid was the Banco de Jagua lying some 25 miles offshore, an unmarked reef with dangerous seas and numerous wrecks. Clear of dangers, there was light airs and calms. The 2nd night was weird, there was lots of phosphorescence and the sea so flat and glassy that the stars were reflected in it. I was dozing below when the wind returned, at last we could make progress. I spotted the island, a low smudge on the horizon just before noon and later in the afternoon I picked up a mooring at Scott's Anchorage, Cayman Brac. This is one of the Cayman Islands.

The authorities came to meet me on the dock and were going to come out to the boat to complete formalities but looking at the size of my dinghy decided to do it ashore. I just had to ferry the mosquito control officer out to spray the inside of the boat.

Ashore later it was in a bit of culture shock, there was a supermarket with everything you could wish for. After months of very basic stores and not being able to get things this was wonderful and of course English was the language, no more struggling to get by in Spanish or French as I had for months.

Both the islands are small, about 9 miles long by 2 wide, about 1,500 people live on Cayman Brac whilst on Little Cayman the resident population is about 150, the people are very friendly.

Exploring Cayman Brac I was offered a lift and was taken along to the Bat cave, fascinating but I saw no bats. Walking back I visited Rebecca's cave then hiked across the salt pond trail back to the north side of the island, hard going this across tortured sharp eroded limestone, in flip flops too, not the best footwear for this terrain.

Next day I sailed across to Little Cayman, I thought to take a mooring in Spot Bay but discovered the dock there, old and concrete, was too high to land on from a dinghy. I moved on around to Owens Sound, entered through a very narrow gap in the reef with breaking waves either side, scary. Once inside it was calm but very shallow, around 2 metres with shoal patches. I was pleased to be in and secured to a stout mooring buoy.

Little Cayman is famous for its iguanas, what wonderful beasts they are, iguanas everywhere I looked. Stopping at a respectful distance one big one about 4 ft long eyed me up and then came across, stopping about 2 ft short of me.

I rode my bike around the island, about 20 miles but it felt longer, traffic count 2 cars 4 iguanas. Stopping off at Sandy point there was a beautiful white sandy beach with an azure sea protected by a fringing reef. I had the place to myself for a lovely swim.

It blew hard in the early morning with torrential rain, I had a bit of a fright when the anchor alarm went off. I thought the mooring might be dragging so found myself stark naked in the rain and dark putting out the anchor, it washed the salt off me I suppose. Turned out it was just the long scope on the mooring.

Leaving through the reef was worrying with a swell running in from the south after the blow, just line up the range markers astern, aim for the middle of the small gap between marker post and buoy and then for that gap in the breakers outside, safely out phew!

Back on Cayman Brac I cycled and walked up the coast to the Brac, a big limestone cliff, home of many caves and walked up the lighthouse steps to Thomas's cave, used as a hurricane shelter by the locals. I hiked part of the trail through the parrot reserve, but I didn't see any parrots.

I could have stayed longer on these delightful peaceful islands but I wanted to visit Jamaica before heading out of the hurricane zone.

The locals in a bar told me they had heard that bad weather, a northwesterly was due the next night. They were a bit incredulous saying that they just don't get that sort of weather this time of year. I decided to clear out anyway since there are no protected anchorages here and I should be well away from the island by the time it arrived. I left at first light, by late morning the skies were looking increasing ominous and I confess I was a little worried. We soon had torrential rain and thunder. Still I had plenty of searoom, about 100 miles away lay Jamaica so I could afford to heave to and ride anything out if necessary. Later we were hit by a big squall, boy did it blow 35 - 40 knots and such torrential rain as I have never seen. It was awesome, still Sea Bear ploughed on course whilst I sheltered on the companionway steps, raingear on just in case. It did pass and the wind drop but the skies were still dark and full of rain. A migrating swallow joined me seeking shelter from the storm and settled down to roost. Later after dark the wind shifted through 180 degrees as the front passed, the skies started to clear a little and the odd star appeared, the worst seemed to be over. Just after dawn the swallow left.

A tanker bound for Houston passed, rare to see another boat in these waters. So the day gradually passed and I was joined by another swallow on passage who rested awhile perched on the pushpit. Another night and now I could see the loom of the lights of Jamaica. By dawn the coast was revealed and late morning saw me anchored opposite Montego Bay Yacht club, after a passage of 121 miles.

The yacht club were welcoming and I spent a few days here, visiting the Hip Strip, a tourist haunt and the town. It's a town of two parts, inclusive hotels, tourist shops and gated residential developments and the town, all noise, smells, bustle, crowds, street stalls. I enjoyed a visit to the Pork Pit, not an eatery for those of a vegetarian bent. Vast amounts of jerk pork and chicken barbecued on huge barbecues and eaten under a 300 year old cotton tree out the back.

Only about 50 miles down the coast was Ocho Rios but against the wind and current it took more than 24 hours and lots of tacking to get there. This was another place that was very tourist orientated with big hotels and private beaches but the local part of town was interesting. I cleared out the morning a big cruise ship arrived in the bay. Another hard journey against wind and current eastwards to Port Antonio. Eventually passing the Blue Mountains, very beautiful and well named and finally turned in to the twin bays of Port Antonio and picked up a mooring off the Errol Flynn Marina.

This place was much more to my liking, no tourists, no big hotels, no cruise ships. A very beautiful place nestled up to the foot of the Blue Mountains, a well sheltered bay and a nice little town, just local Jamaican life, lots to see and do.

One day I took a bus to Kingston, the road going through the mountains, steep wooded hillsides, gorge like valleys. I got off in downtown Kingston by mistake, it was even a bit much for this intrepid traveler. I have never seen a fight before by bus loaders over poaching customers - real gangster stuff. I went to the Bob Marley museum in his old house, a little bit of a pilgrimage really.

Another day I took a bus along the coast to Boston Bay, reputedly the place for the best jerk pork in Jamaica. A lovely crescent shaped cove of a bay with a sandy beach so I had a lovely swim followed by jerk pork, beer some rum and later another swim, a great day.

In Port Antonio I became quite friendly with the owner of a little beer and rum shack on the corner entrance to what the locals called back central, the entrance to the market. Opposite was like smokers corner with a wonderful array of characters and the sweet smell of ganga in the air, all quite open. I had some good conversations about Jamaica and its problems. One evening they set up a sound system nearby which was great until the police turned up in flak jackets with automatic rifles - they didn't have a permit apparently.

Labour day is a big holiday and they had a big named sound system set up at Bikini Beach, just near where the boat was moored. I went along in the evening, it was quite an experience, sound blaring out and the girls mostly dressed in not much shaking their booty and rum flowing.

It was rainy month in Jamaica so we had plenty of rain, generally soon over but I had a day and night of rain with plenty of thunder and lightening, perhaps a reminder that the season was getting on. Time to head south out of the hurricane zone.

16. How I set off for Curacao and ended up in Panama

"No matter how important a man at sea may consider himself, unless he is fundamentally worthy the sea will some day find him out." (Felix Riesenberg)

And no before I start it wasn't a navigation error.

I had decided after much consideration of the alternatives to go to Curacao to lay up the boat for the hurricane season, I even booked some storage there. Curacao is about 600 miles southeast of Jamaica so I knew it would be a hard passage to windward but I thought it do-able, but just how hard I was later to discover. The forecast looked OK, what they don't tell you however is that passage forecasts of grib files ignore what they term as local disturbances and there was one just to the southeast of Jamaica right then. When I left the weather was fine until later when I ran into this disturbance. Dark rain squall clouds, 30 knots plus of wind, 12ft swells and torrential rain capped with thunder and lightning. It was not pleasant. The wind eased but throughout the first night the skies looked very threatening and lightning flashed all around. By mid morning next day conditions were better but the seas were big so it was hard work punching into them and the motion of the boat was far from relaxing, lots of crashing and lurching.

Thereafter I had a couple of reasonable days but noon to noon runs were disappointing in terms of distance covered, then it was more squalls and a wild night. By the 6th day out I was concerned over our slow progress, the weather which was continuing unsettled and the sea state which was rough.

4.00 am on the 8th day was the final turning point, Curacao still 250 miles away to the southeast on a course of 118 degrees. Hard on the wind the boat was pointing 130 degrees but our course over the ground was 187 degrees so a little west of south. This was due to leeway, the waves and the strong west setting equatorial current, speed over the ground a dismal 0.7 knots. It was pretty obvious even to a stubborn skipper that we weren't going to make Curacao.

An American who I had meet in Jamaica had been selling me on the virtues of Panama, he had been keeping his boat there for the past 8 years. So I decided to head there. It was about 420 miles away but importantly downwind. As soon as I altered course the difference was appreciable, gone the crashing and jerking, the motion although still lively was much more comfortable and boat speed shot up.

The weather though had not done with us yet, after a reasonable day in which we ran 90 miles noon to noon, the night grew steadily wilder and by dawn I was putting the 3rd reef in the main then handed it a bit later when the wind passed 30 knots and the seas were huge, all a bit scary. There was little else to do but put the washboards in the companionway, close the hatch and lie down on a bunk.

By noon it was easing and we could raise more sail, the trouble was the wind continued to drop first to 10 - 13 knots and then next day down to 6 knots and then calm. Now us sailors, we are never happy, there is always either a deal too much wind or not enough. 11 days out and I had to resort to motoring. That was OK for some hours until the engine started to falter and then die. It sounded like fuel starvation to me and the problem was soon traced to a blocked air vent pipe to the fuel tank. Confirmed when I undid the fuel tank filler cap and there was a great rush of air in. For good measure I cleaned out the fuel filter and separator just in case there was water in the fuel, bled the system and we were running again.

In the late afternoon of our 12th day out we sited land off to our port side. I had a bit of a scare that night when a sailboat appeared close by, no AIS, no lights showing, all sails up and fluttering but obviously moving under engine. A powerful light flashed over it brought no response at all and I had to take evading action. The morning of our 13th day on passage I had a fleeting visit from a high speed big black rib crewed by men in black with machine guns. I gave them a cheery wave from the cockpit and satisfied they veered off. Just the Panamanian border force on patrol. The border with Columbian is not far away and drug smugglers obviously a concern. Later we closed the rocks and light on Farallon Sucio and shortly after passed between Isla Verde and the rocks of Bajosalmedio to enter the bay of Portabelo, Panama. It was so good to see green hillsides again. I finally anchored off one of the old forts and the little town of Portabelo. A passage of 835 miles.

Portabelo is a small historical city, part of the Spanish Main (Cartagena/Portobelo/San Lorenzo) and quite interesting. Portobelo was allegedly named by Christopher Columbus in 1502 as Puerto Bello and the city was established in 1586 as a Caribbean transhipment centre for the South American riches the Spaniards looted and took back to Spain. The treasure house is still there and it is said that they once took out all the silver and stacked it in the streets to make room for all the gold. Also dating from the Spanish is a cathedral which is renowned for its black Christ statue.

The jungle has reclaimed some of the fortifications but some have been cleared and the canons are still there, still laying where they were abandoned all those years ago.

Portobelo is also the burial place of Sir Frances Drake, the 16th century English explorer who was buried at sea off Drake's island.

The bay is beautiful, surrounded by wooded hills with humming birds and parrots. I realised that there was more to Panama than just the canal and that the area would bear closer exploration.

Despite Portobelo being a designated port of entry I was having trouble with the formalities. Even after two visits to immigration I still had not been given an entry stamp. They did not like it that my clearance papers from Jamaica had Curacao as my destination. I had explained my diversion and the reasons for it and written them a statement but they were being difficult and would not stamp my passport, saying that I had to visit immigration in Colon. So I decided to go to Shelter Bay near Colon and since it was the rainy season anyway, thought I might haul out, lay the boat up and go back to UK. So early one morning, having put all arrangements in place I weighed anchor and set off along the coast towards Colon. Shelter Bay is situated inside the Colon breakwater, which protects the entrance to the Panama Canal so closing it it was busy with many ships, some at anchor and some on the move and permission has to be sought over VHF from the harbour authorities to enter. Permission granted I passed inside the breakwater and motored to the marina. They were ready for me so I went straight into the haul out dock. Paper work was soon completed and soon Sea Bear was ashore and shored up in the yard.

The marina is on the site of what was the American jungle warfare training centre Fort Sherman so is surrounded by jungle which is slowly reclaiming most of the old military buildings.

The marina had a free bus service which ran into Colon so Monday morning first thing I was on the bus, crossing the canal at one of the Gatun locks. As well as sorting out my entry stamp with immigration I had to get my cruising permit sorted. I'll not bore you with the details suffice it to say it took me from 09.30 until 14.00, visits to 2 different offices, numerous forms to fill in, photocopies to submit and 2 taxi rides across town. Bureaucracy is alive and well in Panama and there is still a market for Tippex. Colon has a bad reputation for muggings and it is not advised for gringos to walk in certain parts of the town, hence the taxi. One good thing though, the women in the shipping office advised me that the fare should be no more than 2$, the taxi driver said well the fare for tourists is 2$ but for locals 1$, I'll charge you 1$. The drive was interesting, chaotic traffic but I have never seen such a run down city in all my travels, it was a bit shocking really.

A few days later with Sea Bear safely laid up, a flight took me to the UK.

17. Panama, Guna Yala and the canal

"If we are always arriving and departing, it is also true that we are eternally anchored. One's destination is never a place but rather a new way of looking at things." (Henry Miller)

I arrived back at Sea Bear in Panama in December 2016, the temperature was in the 30's, a bit of a shock after cold England. It took me a few days to get acclimatised but nevertheless it was great to just pull a pair of shorts and a vest on and begin the task of fitting out. This was slow going in the heat and I had a few problems to solve. One was a crack in the heel of the keel which had to be ground out and repaired. It turns out a few Vancouver 28s have suffered this fault, the two parts are just glued together and not bonded over with glass fibre. Fortunately it turned out to be just a surface crack so there was no water ingress in the moulding.

The boat yard is surrounded by jungle so between jobs I took walks, and saw some of the wildlife. I didn't see any jaguars, sloths or toucans but did see nasua narica, a monkey, great kisadees, tropical king birds, hummingbirds, greater ani and vultures, the last beautiful in flight but ugly and awkward on the ground.

After re-launching I had a disaster afternoon. There was a drain valve at bottom of fuel tank, just checking things over it looked like it was leaking a bit, investigating and it fell off in my hand so there I was laying in the engine bay with my finger stopping the hole where once the valve was. Like the Dutch boy and the dam trying to stop 30 gallons of diesel pouring into the bilges. Mmm I thought! Anyway someone heard me shouting and came to help so I was able to tell them where a wooden plug and a hammer was so I hammered a plug in the hole for a temporary fix.

The reducer between tank and valve had been just a mild steel fitting, not fit for purpose at all and had just corroded away. Lucky that it had happened here where I was able to fix it and not somewhere out at sea. I managed to get the tank pumped out, the fitting replaced with new valve and the tank refilled.

Leaving Shelter Bay in January, I wanted to visit the Guna Yala or San Blas islands, first stop Portobelo. The clearwater buoy marking the entrance to the bay had disappeared since June, probably a victim of Otto and in the bay there were several wrecked boats. Otto being the late season hurricane that had hit the coast further north, the latest and furthest south hurricane ever recorded.

Another teething problem surfaced, this a hole in the heads outlet pipe spraying out dirty water! Though how a hole had suddenly appeared in a 4mm thick reinforced pvc pipe beats me. Shortening the pipe by cutting off the end fixed it but what a struggle to get the pipe back on - it took about 3 hours!

On to Isla Linton, the entrance was spectacular between surf on the reef on one hand and crashing waves on the rocks on the other hand. In the morning I dinghied across to the island, I didn't make much progress into the jungle though. Returning towards the beach I was just sheltering from a rain shower under a palm tree, I turned around and there were 2 monkeys sitting behind me not 2 feet away. They walked with me back to the beach, I was amazed at how upright they walked. One grabbed me around the legs, I was just a bit wary as had been warned they sometimes bite and this one was obviously thinking of some monkey business.

Whilst at anchor here the weather continued unsettled, always strong winds, some heavy rain squalls and one knew the waves outside this sheltered inlet would be big.

Eventually the winds eased so it became more favourable for making the passage eastwards to Guna

Yala. A long tack north out to sea then I could tack east. I think 15 knots is my favourite sailing breeze, light enough to set all plain sail to make reasonable progress, not too strong to kick up much of a sea.

By early afternoon I put into Green Turtle bay. It was too rolly to stay but I could prepare a meal before weighing anchor in the early evening and set off for a night passage.

Another long tack northwards away from the coast before tacking east again. The trick I find is to be far enough offshore not to worry about inshore shoals and danger but not too far so you are playing with the big boys, the tankers and container ships. Dawn saw me within sight of Punta San Blas. I had planned on anchoring at Chichame Cays but on approach it looked a bit crowded so I carried on. However aiming for the Eden Channel I got a bit of a scare when I got the islands confused, went off line and strayed over a shoal patch. Maybe I was too tired and dim witted after the night passage with no sleep. I headed back to Chichame and entered the lagoon, it was busy but there was enough room and I anchored, time for some rest.

Beautiful though it was here, sandy palm treed islands, it was a bit like westerners doing their 'being on holiday' thing. So next day I went in search of the real Guna Yala. I anchored off the island of Acuadup.

Ashore was a traditional Guna village, palm leaf thatched huts, Guna indians in native dress, lots of dugout canoes. I bought some bread.

Moving on next day I passed through the well populated and busy Carti islands. I went to Soledad Mira, another traditional village and anchored. Unfortunately the holding here was not good, I was anchored on a small sloping boulder shelf, so I left after a while and went to Los Grullos, anchoring off Kuandiup, just another sandy palm tree island. On to Mokame, a populated traditional island. Here I spent some time talking with a Guna guide who told me of some of their traditions, beliefs, and of the shaman. He showed me around the village, the meeting hut or congresso, his hut and his Nuchus. These are small carved wooden statues, a link between the physical and spiritual side of life. I bought a lobster from a passing fisherman in his dugout canoe. They free dive to catch these by hand, quite impressive. Cooked up it made a delicious meal.

The Guna Indians live on the islands because they are free from insects and other things in the jungle on the mainland but they tend gardens in the jungle for their produce, paddling over there in their dugout canoes.

On then to Salardup an island in the Naguarandup Cays, a group of mostly uninhabited islands scattered along a 6 mile long barrier reef, further offshore than the inhabited islands. Salardup is in a lagoon approached through a gap in the surrounding reef. None of the reefs in the San Blas are marked, mark one eyeball navigation is required for spotting the colour of the water to show you the depth.

I completed a circumnavigation of sorts of the Naguarandup Cays, sailing down the inland channel then out past Kanlildup or Green Island towards the Coca Bandera Cays then back westwards to the Lemmon Cays to anchor between three islands with a very shallow approach. A long days sailing through beautiful islands, so many islands. Some fishermen came alongside and offered me some fish, nice and fresh and still wriggling about in the bottom of their boat. So that was the problem of what to eat for dinner solved.

I left Lemmon Cays soon after first light, as soon as the light was good enough to see the reefs. Out past the reefs and breaking surf I could set a course to clear the reefs of Porvener. A close reach this, wind about 20 knots and a reasonably lively sea. I chose to get enough northing in to clear all offshore dangers meaning I could run down my westing free in that knowledge, rather like the old time clippers used to do. Once out at 9 degrees 38 minutes I turned westwards, putting Sea Bear on a beam reach and she fairly romped along. Much later the average speed on the log was showing 6.1 knots, good going indeed for us. Rounding Isla Tamba and Isla Grande we were in good time and so instead of going in to Isla Linton to anchor I carried on to Portobelo. The wind had eased a little over the last hour but rounding Drake Island and within sight of the anchorage with the log showing 60 miles covered in 10 hours, it died completely. No problem I thought I'll just motor the last mile to anchor, but problem there was. The engine did not start, it would not even turn over but was locked solid. An initial assessment showed me that it wasn't something I could fix right then. I knew that it couldn't be seized as it had ran fine that morning. I suspected that the engine had somehow filled with water and had a hydraulic lock. With wind I could have sailed in but there was none. I called up some cruisers in the bay over the vhf and explained my position so they said they would come out in their dinghies and assist. Before they arrived though a little breeze came back so I sailed towards the anchorage, the dinghies dully arrived and shepherded me to anchor. I was grateful for their support.

Safely at anchor it was out with the tools, out with the injectors, off with the exhaust elbow and drain all the seawater out of the engine and crank by hand to blow the remains out. I put it all back together and mercifully the engine started and ran. I warmed it up to drive out any moisture lingering. I finished well after dark and then I could make a cuppa and cook dinner.

Puzzling over why this had happened I investigated further and discovered the air inlet pipe to the anti-syphon valve was blocked, allowing sea water to syphon in to the exhaust manifold and thence the engine. Easily solved that but worse was that the exhaust elbow was corroded inside - the only cure for that a new one.

I spent a couple of day at Portobelo then headed off to Shelter Bay, it turned out to be a very windy day and approaching the breakwater we had rain squalls too. Dodging both and outgoing and ingoing big ships I entered the breakwater and so to moor alongside in Shelter Bay marina. Time to try and get a new exhaust elbow. I had been undecided for some while about whether I was going to transit the Panama canal or not to the Pacific. Even after all these miles of single-handing, it was a fairly daunting prospect. Quite a step up in terms of distance and commitment but I had made the decision so I had best make a start with the canal paperwork.

Before leaving Portobelo I had completed and emailed in form 4405-i, the first step in registering your boat in the Panama canal system and requesting a transit. I had decided to do the process myself rather than using an agent.

Initial enquiries about getting a new exhaust elbow in Panama seemed to suggest I might have to wait 2 weeks or more but I found a guy in America who made them in stainless steel so I ordered one from him. It took a week, 3 days to get from Virginia to Panama City via New York then 4 days to get from Panama City the 70 k to Colon, where I collected it from the Post Office. That was quite an experience in itself, 3 different counters to visit and different forms to fill and sign for, then the packet was given to the Customs official who spent most of time sitting dozing on a chair, he opened it to check that its contents matched the description on the customs form. That same day I also visited Citibank to check that they had received my canal transit fees through wire transfer and completed the last bit of paperwork. On to the supermarket for more provisions, stocking up for the long haul.

Back at the boat the new exhaust elbow was fitted and the engine run up - all good to go.

Earlier in the week I had arranged for an admeasurer from the canal to come and measure the boat and I had completed all the necessary forms to request a handline transit of the canal. The final step was to phone up the scheduler for a transit slot. I was given Friday 17th Feb.

I would have to be at the Flats anchorage to pick up my transit advisor at 14.00 then shortly afterwards motor the 4 miles to the Gatun locks. After the 3 locks you moor up for the night in Gatun lake before resuming the rest of the transit the next morning.

With a date assigned I phoned Tito to hire the necessary lines 4 x 150ft 7/8" to 1" lines and heavy duty fenders. Now to find 4 line-handlers.

A few days before my own scheduled transit I went through the canal as a line handler on Philip's boat Wandering Star, a 45' Irwin ketch. The other line handlers were an English couple from Morpheus, my neighbours on the pontoon in Shelter Bay and a young Panamanian, Carlos. Late afternoon and we picked up the transit advisor at the Flats anchorage and motored to the Gatun locks. Before entering we rafted up with a catamaran in the centre, us to starboard and a big pilot house ketch to port. The Panamanian canal line handlers ashore threw us hauling lines weighted with monkeys fists, we attached the mooring warps to them, we were walked into the lock and once in place the line-handlers ashore dropped the loops over bollards and the line-handlers on the boats took up the slack. Lock doors closed and water flooded in, the turbulence was considerable, there was a lot of strain on the lines and taking in the lines as the raft rose was hard. There are 3 Gatun locks and we passed from one to the other with the line-handlers ashore casting us off and walking us through to the next lock. Going through at the same time was a big freighter in front of us, they have only a few feet clearance either side so move very slowly, guided by the mules (electric locomotives) to which they are tied so it all took some time. By the time we were through the 3rd lock and could de-raft it had already been dark for some time and we motored to anchor near the designated mooring buoy to spend the night in Gatun Lake. Our transit advisor left us and we could settle down to eat and drink a few beers.

Resuming the transit the next morning with a new advisor, we motored across the lake then through the cuts past Gamboa and through the Gaillard cut, past Gold hill, under the Centenario bridge and so to the San Pedro lock where the descent to the Pacific begins. Rafting up again we entered the lock, this time in front of a freighter. Down-locking is much more gentle with no turbulence. On through the Minaflores lake to the 2 Minaflores locks and then finally to the Pacific. Just a few more miles and under the Bridge of the Americas and there is Balboa Yacht Club with its moorings. The club boatman ran us ashore and we said our farewells to Philip and taxied back to Shelter Bay. It was a worthwhile experience and had prepared me for my own transit.

For my transit I enlisted the English crew of Tintin, recently arrived and scheduled to transit a few days later. Motoring out of the marina Sea Bear felt heavy and sluggish with 5 aboard. At the flats waiting for the advisor I talked through the procedure with the crew and when the advisor arrived we set off for the locks.

Sea Bear was rafted alongside 2 big yachts and the advisors said the 2 big yachts would do all the line handling and manoeuvring. We were just grateful passengers and so had an easy time of it. Passing through the Gatun locks was quicker this time so we were moored up to the big buoy before dark. Dinner was cooked and eaten and some beers drunk. Now Sea Bear has only 3 bunks so I slept in the cockpit and another elected to sleep on the foredeck. It was a fine night fortunately.

The advisor had warned that they would be early next morning and indeed Larry, our new advisor turned up at 6.45 and we were off. Tea was already brewed so I let one of the crew helm whilst I cooked breakfast for all. When doing your transit application you must specify your cruising speed, I had specified 5 knots, this is the minimum speed allowed. I was little concerned at being able to maintain this especially so heavily laden as we were but we averaged 5.7 for the next 5 hours that we took to motor the 28.6 miles across the lake and to the

San Pedro lock, where we arrived at 11.45. The lake is quite beautiful with lots of tree covered islands, on the biggest of which is the Smithsonian Tropical research station. We did this time see a crocodile basking in the shallows of one island.

Down-locking this time was quite quick, no big freighter to wait for. Rafted together again with Arielle, and a French Onvi, we locked through with a big sail training ship and a passenger ferry. Exiting the San Pedro lock we spotted another crocodile. Shortly after 2pm our advisor was picked up and we t tied up to a mooring buoy at Balboa Yacht club. It had been an easy and stress free transit.

I went ashore in the club boat with my crew and dropped of the tyre fenders (3$ each to hire 1$ each to drop off). The crew of Arielle were at the yacht club and we drank some beer before they went off in the taxi that we had pre-arranged back to Shelter Bay.

Connected up to wifi I discovered that John Whittle, an old friend and work associate from my time as a climbing guide had suddenly died. So no joy at being through to the Pacific. The day ended on a sombre note and I drank the last of my beer in remembrance of him.

I spent a few days at the Balboa Yacht Club moorings, I had been led to believe that they were very rolly with wakes from big ships but I found this not to be the case at all. Making final preparations for the Pacific I spent some time visiting several chandlers but I couldn't get all the bits I wanted which I found a bit surprising in such a big place. I did in the course of my wandering use the Metro subway, very fast and efficient in addition to taxis and the metro bus. I did get a chart for Tonga which I was missing and a new Nautical almanac from Islamoradora the excellent chart agents in Balboa.

I went to the open air vegetable market at Abastos which was huge and bought lots of good quality un-refrigerated fruit and vegetables which keep much better than cold stored supermarket ones for the journey. Another purchase was a new windup kitchen timer - just the thing to time your catnaps at sea, though I won't be able to doze with it on my chest as used to be my wont with my old one as it it egg shaped and so would roll off.

To complete departure formalities an international zarpe was got from the port captain at Flamenco and immigration visited.

I went to get diesel topped up and whilst moored up to the fuel barge some clot in a work boat who was moored astern decided for some unknown reason to reverse into me. There was a horrible noise and the wind vane paddle was horribly bent. I was fuming as you might imagine. The design of the monitor wind vane self steering is such that there is a sacrificial tube between paddle and gear mechanism and it was this that was bent. I do carry a spare but I wasn't about to tell the other boat that. A yacht club official on the fuel dock was helpful, taking all the details. I took off the paddle and stripped out the tube giving it to the guy on the dock who said he would insist it was fixed today as he knew I was leaving. I went back to the mooring to wait. They came by later but it was still not quite straight so he went away again. They came back later with a new one which was a better result and I had also got the old one which is not quite straight but will do as another spare at a pinch. Putting it back on involved some slightly dodgy sitting perched over the water on the back framework.

I was all ready now but I needed a beer, after all it would be last one for a while.

First stop was planned for Las Perlas islands then it would out into the Pacific proper for the long haul.

18. Las Perlas and passage to Galapagos

"The sea has never been friendly to man. At most it has been the accomplice of human restlessness." (Joseph Conrad)

I left Balboa moorings at first light and after motoring out of the channel set a course for the Las Perlas, a cluster of over 20 mainly uninhabited islands about 40 miles away. There was little wind so mainly motoring until later on when I picked up a southerly breeze. I eventually anchored off the northwest coast of La Contadora, the busiest of the islands, a weekend retreat for rich Panamanians. Next day I moved on to a lovely anchorage in the channel between Isla Espiritu Santo and the main island of Isla Del Rey. Supposedly a popular anchorage but I had it all myself, it was very peaceful, there was lots of pelicans and parrots. Now I could start the task of diving under and ensuring the hull was clean before passage and that afternoon I got one side done but I found it tiring work. I was wanting to finish the job off next morning but the tide was running swiftly past the boat and I decided it wouldn't be wise. Yes welcome back to tides, something you almost forget about in the Caribbean, here the range is about 15 ft. I therefore moved on, motoring down the east side of the islands to almost the southern end. Here I anchored at Rio Cacique which the pilot book assured me you were almost certain to find flat water. So it was and I finished off the hull cleaning.

A quick dive next morning as a final check then it was time to leave, there was at least some wind and from the north so I set off for the long passage bound for the Galapagos. Probably like many other cruisers I had some regrets at not having more time to spend exploring in these delightful islands but the Pacific beckoned.

I did have a calm patch passing through the wide gap between Isla Galera and Punta Gorda but then the wind was back. A notable sight was the sting rays jumping vertically from the water, turning end over end and landing with an almighty splash. It is a mystery even to marine biologists why they do this.

So the day passed and the first night, I saw lots of big ships bound to and from Panama but all a good distance off. I was off to a flying start because in the first 24 hours Sea Bear had run 130 miles. However it was not to last and the winds grew lighter and lighter with some periods of calm. I don't think I saw winds over 8 knots again. So the days passed, once clear of the shipping channel there were no ships and little to do apart from ring the changes with the sails, pole out the yankee opposite to the main, lets try the cruising chute, the occasional gybe to keep on course as far as possible, a little tweak to the self steering now and again. On the 8th day I was a little surprised to see a fishing vessel it must be 200 miles at least from the nearest land. The 7th March, 9th day out was a memorable day in that just after 6pm we crossed the equator, no visitation from Neptune but I had a tot of rum by way of celebration. The GPS told me we had 120 miles to San Cristobel. After sunset and a big bird made a determined effort to land atop the mast, succeeding after several attempts. I guessed it must be a land bird as a sea bird would surely just settle on the water, but I wasn't able to identify it. It perched there all night leaving with first light in the morning.

My patience with these calms and light winds was wearing thin so on nightfall of day 10 when it fell calm and there was about 50 miles to Isla San Cristobal I resorted at last to the engine. It didn't help that the auto pilot had packed up so hand steering it was. The wind did return for a while but not for long and when it died again I let the boat drift and took a 30 minute nap before turning on the engine again. It had been a lovely full bright moon night but eventually it sunk below a thick band of clouds so it was really dark. Now I knew there was an island somewhere hereabouts, but just where?. First light and all was revealed and I was shortly entering Wreck Bay to anchor. It had been 10 days short 1 hour for the 838 mile passage.

I was a little surprised how green was the island after all I had read. There was plenty of trees and vegetation, but then I suppose it was the rainy season.

First thing after anchoring was a dive over the side to check the bottom of Sea Bear, it had accumulated a crop of goose barnacles so those were scraped off. A big boxy fish, a puffer fish came along to help, tugging them off and eating them.

Formalities took some time to complete, it all has to be done through an agent. At one time there were 6 officials aboard plus a diver inspecting the hull. It was all very friendly though and no problems although expensive, I just had to be fumigated in the morning. For that I had to be off the ship for 3 hours so I explored the town, watched the sea lions, swam at the beach and found a nice restaurant for a 4$ fish meal.

Subsequent days saw me walk to the nearby beaches and to La Loberia for my first sight of marine iguanas, more sea lions of course, this place is ruled by sea lions. Birds including the famed finches, a lava heron, white checked pintails, oystercatcher, a plover and of course plenty of pelicans and frigate birds.

Another day I took the bus, they only run on a Sunday, across the island passing through the farming area of El Progresso to La Galapaguera, a breeding project for giant tortoises. A walk around here and then on to Puerto Chino, the end of the road and a walk to another lovely beach for a swim. No sign of a bus back so after a long wait I rode back in the back of a pickup truck which is what all the taxis here are.

Boat maintenance carried on, this time it was major re-stitch of the seams of the spray hood where the stitching had either frayed through or was rotted by sunlight and sea air. It was hard awkward work.

There is only the one road so some days later I rode my bike up past the highest point, Cerro San Joaquin (896m) to El Junco where I walked up to see the crater lake. That was some hard ride but it was much easier freewheeling back downhill. I got soaked in a downpour but you don't get cold here near the equator so it barely matters.

Leaving Sea Bear at anchor I took a launcha, a fast motorboat with 3 big outboard engines that do the 40 mile trip in about 2 hours over to Puerto Ayora, Santa Cruz to meet up with my son Ged who flown into the Galapagos. We visited the Darwin centre and walked to Turtle bay. The birds here were amazingly tame and unafraid, perching on Ged's chest whilst he was sunbathing and eating crumbs from his hand. We then managed to arrange a few days on a tourist boat. This was very good indeed, the food superb and the wildlife guide very knowledgable and informative. We visited giant tortoises in the highlands of Santa Cruz then the boat took us overnight to the island of Espanola. Here we walked ashore at Gardner bay for sea lions and marine iguanas, and snorkeled in the bay seeing turtles. On then to Punta Suarez for a walk across the peninsular through marine iguana breeding sites and masked booby colonies. Even though it was a little early in the season we were lucky to see one waved albatross. One of the features of the Galapagos is the fearless nature of all the wildlife meaning that you can approach really close which is very special. Here we also saw the Galapagos hawk.

Next was the island of Santa Fe for the cactus trees and land iguanas found only on this island. Then to South Plaza, a different type of landscape, a different type of iguanas plus nesting on the cliffs swallow tail gulls, blue footed boobies and Audubon's shearwaters. Throughout there were frigate birds, tropic birds, finches, mockingbirds and Galapagos doves.

Tour finished we bussed over Santa Cruz to Puerto Ayora and Ged and I returned by launcha to San Cristobal to rejoin Sea Bear.

We had a fabulous snorkel in a rocky cove underneath Cerro Tijeretas with big schools of fish, many brightly coloured big fish and with sea lions swimming really close to you. This can be a trifle scary, they are so big and fast and zoom past, it is a good job that they are not aggressive.

But my time in the Galapagos was up, Ged left to go back to UK. It had been fabulous, but it was time to arrange my zarpe, clear immigration, stock up with water, vegetables, fruit and bread and head on out for the Marquesas. They were about 3,000 miles away so I expected the passage would take me 30 days or more.

19. Passage to Marquesas

"The first experience can never be repeated. The first love, the first sunrise, the first South Sea Island, are memories apart, and touch a virginity of sense." (Robert Louis Stevenson)

I had a, what I think to be a very slow passage, following just about the great circle route which differs not a lot in these latitudes from the rhumb route. I'll not bore you with the full details but I can understand why Connor O'Brien, who was the first Irish yacht circumnavigator, said if he had to sail 5,000 miles in the trade winds he would die of boredom. Still as the great Moitessier said, cruising is one long game of patience.

I'll just add trade winds what trade winds! The pilot books had assured me I would be gently wafted from Galapagos to the Marquesas by the southeast trades.

Leaving the Galapagos I had no wind then a succession of squalls, one which caught me unawares on a grey drizzly morning when the wind went from 10 knots to 35 - 40 in a matter of moments and torrential rain. It was one of those scary moments which bought to me how alone you are out there and far away from any help. It would after one of these squalls that one morning I noticed several rips in the staysail. This was a bit of a blow, I did patch it but it dint last long. I handed it and replaced it with the storm staysail, a bit small this for normal usage but better than nothing. Then the weather improved for some days but I still had a series of grey overcast days with no sight of the sun. The winds were light, many days of 8 - 9 knots of wind and sometimes lower. At first they were indeed from the southeast, living up to their name in direction at least and we could sail along on a broad reach but then they went east even northeast so it was dead downwind. This is a point of sailing that neither Sea Bear nor I agree to like and there was always enough swell to create at times, lively rolling which was tiresome.

It amazed me how quickly weed and barnacles grow on the bottom in these waters. I had started out clean but after a week there was already a fair growth and it doesn't take too much to slow the boat down and make her sluggish and unresponsive on the helm. One day when the wind was only 3 knots I did launch the dinghy and try and scrape some away but there was too much swell and I adjudged it too dangerous. I also got badly stung on the arm by a jellyfish whilst attempting to clean the bottom. Long gelatinous threads with bright blue specks and of course if you rub the affected area, ones instinctive reaction, it just makes it worse as it spreads the sting around. I later discovered the best treatment is vinegar. It had been my habit every day, whilst naked in the cockpit to tip a bucket or two of sea water over my head. I had never bothered to peer into the bucket before, but following this incident I always carefully inspected the contents of the bucket before tipping it over me.

There is very little boat traffic this way and I only saw 3 boats, one a freighter and two fishing boats, still with a guard alarm set on AIS it did mean I could get some decent sleep. It was on this passage that I started to have trouble with the GPS, it seemed to be working OK in terms of position fixing but the screen was becoming increasing difficult to read. It looked liked the LED screen was failing. I was thankful that I had a spare handheld GPS and of course the AIS to give me a position.

On a long passage like this you can settle into a sot of routine. A mug of tea and breakfast shortly after sunrise, then an inspection round the boat checking for any potential problems like chafe on the rigging or sails, loose shackles, missing split pins. Midday and it is time to mark up the position on the chart, work out the noon to noon run, and fill in the log. I generally ate my evening meal around 5.30 so I could clear up before dark. Just before sunset I would often put a precautionary reef in the main, check everything over and lay out some warmer clothes for the night. Sometime as I watched the sunset I would have a small tot and maybe listen to some music. Then it was on with the navigation lights and dress in warmer clothes. I would half doze maybe with a blanket around me in a corner of the cockpit under the spray hood. Sometimes I would stretch out and sleep wedged sideways across the cockpit, at other times I would retire for a sleep in my bunk. All these activities punctuated by watching the weather and waves and keeping a lookout for shipping. Days merged into one another, only by the log could you keep track of the days. It was a bit like groundhog day and I think I know what it's like to be in limbo now.

The last few hundred miles seemed to take forever. The penultimate day, around midday I spied land, at first I was not quite sure, was it cloud? but no a bit later I was certain - Land Ho! The Marquesas are high mountainous islands and I was still 45 miles off. There was no chance to get in before dark that night so when about 20 miles off I hove to and drifted slowly towards them. Dawn I let draw again, what magnificent islands, steep mountainous, verdant and largely unspoiled.

Later as I turned into Atuona Bay, Hiva Oa, I met with Thom on another Vancouver 28 just leaving. We both hove to and had a good old fashioned gam. It was my first meeting with Thom although we had corresponded via email before.

I anchored in the bay. I had made it to one of the most remote group of inhabited islands in the world, Gauguin's paradise, after a passage of 2995 nautical miles and 34 days.

Always the first job once the boat is securely anchored is to register with the Authorities. A walk of about 3 kilometres took me to the town of Atuona. At the gendamarie I discovered that the time zone here is a half hour different not one hour which is the usual step in time from one zone to another, and the place was shut until after lunch. A visit to an ATM saw me furnished with funds, but I had no idea of the exchange rate, although the Polynesian Franc notes were very colourful and pretty. With a pocket full of money I could have lunch myself at a nearby eatery, a real treat after so long on the boat. I had fresh tuna and the waitress wore a flower in her hair.

Later formalities were initiated very easily, but I had to post the form the gendarmes gave me to Papete, Tahiti where I would have to visit to complete formalities when I got there.

I visited the shops and bought a real treat in the shape of baguettes and french cheese, that would go well with my last bottle of french wine later as a celebration of arrival. Ooh and some tins of cold Tahitian beer, one drunk on the spot, perhaps that's why the walk back to the boat seemed so long.

I spent a few days at Atuona, looking around and enjoying land. It is said that the custom of tattooing originated in the Marquesas and that it was sailors visiting here following the "discovery" of the south sea islands by Europeans who got tattooed and brought tattooing to the west. It seemed somehow appropriate then for me to get a tattoo here in its homeland. So I sought out a local tattoo artist and had a band inked on my arm. His house was adorned with wild boar skulls. There are a lot of wild boars in the forest here which they still hunt the old fashioned way with dogs and spears.

A river emptied into the anchorage bay and it rained a lot meaning the water was very muddy but one benefit of this was that all the fresh water killed off the goose barnacles and weed on the hull.

Leaving Hiva Oa around the full moon, I thought to have a pleasant moonlit sail to the island of Fatu Hiva. At about 45 miles away it was just too far to guarantee managing it all in daylight. It is one disadvantage of sailing in the tropics 12 hour days and 12 hour nights. As it was it turned out to be very cloudy, so there was no moon to light my way.

I arrived in Baie Hanavave or Bay of the Virgins, a truly spectacular anchorage, steep sided and dominated by rock pinnacles and behind a backdrop of steep high mountains. The island is very unspoilt and the people super friendly. I went to a dinner of traditional fare hosted for cruisers by a family from the village. Roast pork, roast goat, breadfruit, coconut milk, roasted pink bananas and pamplemousse was amongst the items on offer.

One day a walk took me to a lovely 200 ft waterfall up the valley behind the village where I skinny dipped in the plunge pool, very refreshing. Another walk took me high above the bay looking down on the boats at anchor.

Leaving Fatu Hiva, another night sail took me to the island of Tahuata where I anchored at Baie Hanamoenoa. This was reckoned by one authority to be one of the three most beautiful anchorages in Polynesia. An uninhabited bay with a yellow sand beach backed by coconut palms and a backdrop of green hills. Very soft and gentle by Marquesian standards I thought.

Next I went to Taiohae bay on the island of Nuka Hiva. This bay is very big and able to accommodate lots of yachts at anchor so is a major gathering point in the Marquesas for cruisers. The town ashore is the biggest in the Marquesas so there are shops, a bank, restaurants etc so it is a good place to re-provision and relax. However all the supplies come in by boat which was due in a few days, in between shipments they do run out of things so for the first few day here the shelves were thinly stocked and they had run out of flour so there was no bread to be had.

Thom was anchored here so it was good to catch up and compare notes on our Pacific passages so far. We also looked over each other boats which although the same model had a few differences in layout and set up. Thom also very kindly lent me his spare staysail until I reached Tahiti so this was a great help. There were also here some other cruisers that I had got to know so it was a fairly sociable time.

Whilst here I took a few local walks and had a second go at repairing my leaky dinghy not entirely successfully.

My next move was to another bay about 5 miles along the coast, Baie Tai'oe. The entrance to this bay was hidden and looked rather improbable at first. Entering between a rocky point with breaking waves and tall vertiginous cliffs and with quite a swell running was a trifle daunting. Once inside though it was sheltered, calm and peaceful and you couldn't even see the ocean.

Thom arrived next day with a new crew member for me, a French girl Marie. I had mentioned the other day when a group of us had a pizza together that I was a bit concerned about passing through the Tuamotus or

Dangerous Archipelago without a crew to watch for reefs and coral heads in the passes and here was a volunteer to come with me.

Beside the spectacular scenery of this bay one of the attractions was reputedly the 3rd highest waterfall in the world being up the valley. It turned out that this claim was far from the truth but it was a spectacular waterfall all the same. Next day I dinghied around to the village of Hakaui, population 10, and walked up the trail to Vaipo falls. The trail was wet and muddy and you had to ford a knee deep fast running river. You were rewarded with a wonderful view at one point before pushing on through the forest. All around were the ruins of ancient paepae or house platforms, at one time the valley must have supported a large population. Indeed when Captain Cook first visited the islands it was reckoned the total population of the islands was around 100,000. The natives had no immunity to diseases bought by western seaman and the high mortality reduced the population to a low point of around 2,500. Nowadays there has been some recovery and the population is some 9,300 spread over the 6 of the inhabited islands in the archipelago.

I got back to the village before it started raining then had an exciting time going back out through the surf to the boat, I thought I might get flipped but just took a wave aboard.

I went back to the village next morning and filled my water cans and bought a whole load of fruit, a hand of bananas, pamplemousse, limes and a breadfruit

We weighed anchor early from Baie Taiohae and set off for the island of Oa Pou about 25 miles away. We were rewarded with blue skies and moderate winds and a fairly calm sea so had a nice sail across.

Oa Pou is very dramatic island with tall rock spires, the tallest is Mt Oave, a volcanic plug at 4,004 feet high. There was hardly any cloud when we approached so we could see them in all their splendour but they soon became coy and hid themselves in clouds.

Hakahau with a population of about a thousand is the 3rd most populated village in the Marquesas, but feels a sleepy little place. We were anchored in the bay behind the breakwater which gives some protection from the swell.

This was our jumping off spot for the Tuamotus about 400 miles away. We had a very windy spell and it kicked up quite a sea outside so we waited for that to settle before making passage, setting off when the weather looked suitable.

We had mixed weather for the 450 mile passage to the Tuamotus with very variable winds in strength and direction from southeast to northeast and 3 days of very cloudy grey conditions. However it was never too windy nor too rough so no complaints on that score. Another passage with no sightings of shipping, no dolphins, no whales and just one fishing boat as we closed on Ahe in the early hours of the last morning. Our trailing of a fishing line proved unsuccessful too. We managed to hook two, both reel screamers, both big but the first just bent the hook and the second broke the line like it was a piece of weak cotton.

The Tuamotus are a large group of around 77 coral atolls and they earned their reputation as the Dangerous Isles because the motus and coral reefs are so low lying and hard to spot. In the past most cruisers avoided them for that reason. We did not sight Ahe until we were about 5 miles away, a thin line of coconut trees fringing the horizon.

On Ahe there is just one pass into the lagoon, about 85 feet wide at its narrowest and just 3-4 metres deep over the bar. Through this rushes all the water in and out of the lagoon with the tides so a slack water passage is recommended. Only having the tide times for another atoll, Rangiroa about 90 miles away we had to guess and rely on the look of the water. Motoring in we had about 2-3 knots of tide against us, so slow progress but plenty of steerage way. Once inside over the bar the current slackened and we could follow the marked channel across the lagoon to anchor off the village of Tenukapara.

Even though Ahe is one of the smaller atolls the lagoon feels vast inside and it is strange to be encircled by all the islets or motus which comprise the rim of the atoll. Strange too that night when the boat was so peaceful on the anchor, so still, no rocking or rolling, it was hard to remember when the boat had last been that quiet aboard, the San Blas Islands I think back in January.

About 100 people live in the village and they were super friendly. I was outside the post office and a women asked if I had any music. She rushed off for a memory card and I put a lot of reggae on it for her. She gave me a whole load of bananas.

After a couple of days we left Ahe in the morning and had to motor, following the channel across the lagoon in the teeth of quite a strong head wind. Marie joked that once out through the pass perhaps there would be no wind and after negotiating the pass through the reef that is the way it turned out to be. We set our course for Rangiroa about 83 miles away. Light winds persisted so it was a slow passage but come the dawn we were about 14 miles off Tiputa Pass, one of two entrances to Rangiroa atoll. Land was not sighted till later about 7 miles away, such is the low-lying nature of these atolls which can make approach quite dangerous.

According to my tide table it should have been about 1 hour after low water when we entered the pass and so should have had the tide with us. Judging by the rips and standing waves I thought and indeed found out otherwise and we had wind against tide making for a fairly exciting entrance of Tiputa pass with Sea Bear surfing down the backs of the waves. It turned out later we impressed a few watching cruisers with our entrance. I later found out that apparently the tide turns maybe 1-2 hours after high or low water, although the tides are very unpredictable and sometimes you get days of outgoing tides at the passes with no inflow at all due to winds and southern swells causing water to flow in over the reefs between the motus in the south of the atoll.

Anyway safely through the pass we were in the lagoon and found a peaceful anchorage off Kia-Ora beach. There were quite a few other boats here unlike Ahe and the atoll was much more touristy.

Swimming around and under the boat here I saw my first Remoras or sharksuckers. These normally attach themselves to sharks with their suckers and fed mainly on host faces. Somehow these two had decided to attach themselves to Sea Bear. They were about two to three feet long and looked rather menacing somehow. It put me off swimming.

After a few days here I set off for Tahiti leaving Marie behind who wanted to spend more time in the atolls. I exited via the other pass, Avaturu and armed with more knowledge had slack water for exit.

Once again I was bedevilled with very light winds as I made my way west along the north of the reefs before turning between Rangiroa and the nearby atoll of Tikehau and setting a course for Tahiti about 180 miles away. In the first 24 hours I made a measly 65 miles and in the dawn light passed the island of Makatea about 12 miles off on the port beam. The afternoon bought better winds and progress was good. Just before sunset I spotted a sail astern, a rare sight for me on passage but it took a long time to overhaul me. Just before dawn the lights of Tahiti were spotted and eventually I entered Papeete harbour and moored alongside a pontoon in Papeete marina. This is in the heart of the town alongside a busy boulevard and quite some change from the anchorages I had been in for the past months. It was much changed since Moitessier's day but it was here that he finally ended his epic 11 month and one and a half times singlehanded circumnavigation of the world.

20. Tahiti

"The wonder is always new that any sane man can be a sailor." (Ralph Waldo Emerson)

Staying at Marina Papeete I was able to complete a few maintenance jobs, chase around after a sailmaker to order a new staysail and get the leaky dinghy repaired, that is as well as a little exploring of the town, dining out at the Roulettes (mobile food vans) at the plaza and quaffing a few beers with friends. Thom from Fathom, Adva from Waterhoen, Oceana and Alice from Danika and Dan from My Dream were all here.

Then it was off to the airport in the early hours to meet Wendy who flew out from UK to join me for a while. I gave her a traditional Tahitian greeting of a garland of flowers.

After a few days we headed to anchor off Maeve beach just a few miles away, a very popular anchorage this off Marina Tanina, with maybe about 150 boats at anchor. My new GPS/plotter arrived to replace the old GPS with burnt out screen, that would make navigation a deal easier.

We had an aborted go at reaching the south of the island, but turned back before exiting the pass in the reef when wind and rain arrived but after a couple of days set out again. We went out through the reef via pass Tappuna with dolphins for company. Sailing south and then turning Pointe de Marua we followed outside the reefs to Teputa pass which we entered and proceeded to anchor at Port du Phaeton. This was a lovely lagoon behind the reef which was so sheltered that it felt like you were anchored in a lake.

Here we tried to visit the Gauguin museum, a few miles along the coast, but it was shut for refurbishment so we contented ourselves with a walk around the botanical gardens there, then back to Tavarao on the bus for a delicious lunch, tuna of course.

After a few days at Port du Phaeton we continued our circumnavigation of Tahiti. First we sailed inside the reef to anchor by Teehupoo, here the road around the island ends. Next day we exited the reef by pass Havae with amazing surf to left and right. Rounding the southeast tip of the island we carried on and once more entered behind the reefs by Passe d' Aiurua and anchored in the lee of a tall cliff by Paofai. There was only a few scattered huts along this coast as the only access is by sea. Carrying on we next stopped after Passe Faatautia. Here the anchorage was very deep, 30 metres and we had to let out all 45m of chain and 40 m of rope rode.

Raising the anchor the next morning without a windlass we resorted to use of a mooring warp tied to the chain with a rolling hitch and led back to the primary winches, 30 m of free hanging chain and an anchor being too heavy to haul or even hold by hand. The reefs in the next section of coast are mostly submerged and harder to spot so we maintained a good offing until we got to Point Venus where we anchored off a beautiful black sand beach in just 6 m. This bay was visited by both the Bounty (before the mutiny) where they raised their cargo of breadfruit plants and before that by Captain Cook. The point derives its name from the observatory set up by Cook to observe the transit of Venus.

Amazingly in the days since Port du Phaeton we saw only 1 other cruising boat, it seems rare these days for cruisers to sail around Tahiti.

Off then for the short sail to Moorea, Tahiti's smaller sister. We anchored just inside the reef at the entrance to Cook's Bay, that man again, a most idyllic spot with water so clear we could see our anchor on the bottom and the occasional passing sting ray. A couple of nights here and we moved to anchor deep within Cooks bay itself amidst most spectacular peaks. We walked up the valley, on a track named the route de Annas, to a pineapple plantation and then continued up well marked trails in the forest. This led past several Mairae (ancient ceremonial platforms) to a viewpoint called the Belvedere from where you could see down into both Cook's bay and Baie d'Opunohu. Carrying on through the forest we came to another wonderful viewpoint of Col des Trois Pines, before returning back to the boat. It was a tiring but well worthwhile day. Truly this is a garden of Eden.

Moving around to Baie d'Opunohu, maybe even more spectacular in scenery than Cook's bay, we anchored inside the reef near the entrance off the small village of Papetoai. We took a long dinghy ride, the channel across too shallow for yachts to an area nicknamed Sting Ray City. Here there is a shallow sandy area frequented by sting rays and reef sharks where you can stand chest deep and snorkel. The local tour guides encourage the rays by feeding them. It was thrilling to swim with these magnificent creatures and feel them brush past you with their wings and allow themselves to be petted.

Sadly our time in Moorea was up and we had to return to Tahiti. The weather had been grand for the past weeks with gentle winds but shortly after exiting the pass through the reef it started to blow. We soon had

30-35 knots of wind which kicked up big waves, a short and horrible breaking sea. Of course it was dead on the nose as well. It was as if the weather was telling us not to leave Moorea and we both wished we could have stayed but Wendy's flight home was the next day so we had to press on. Later the wind eased to about 20-25 knots and then when we were nearing Tahiti dropped away altogether but still leaving of course a sloppy sea. Eventually we were back inside the reef via Papeete harbour and soon past the airport to anchor once more at Maeva Bay near marina Taina. Here we recognised lots of boats still at anchor in the same spots as when we left weeks ago.

With Wendy returning to the UK it was back to single handing.

I took delivery of my new staysail and very good it looked but being so new the material was stiff and slippery so it was going to be difficult to handle for a while.

21. The Iles Sous le Vent

"The sea road is not the safe and easy road." (T.C. Lethbridge)

Before leaving Tahiti I caught a bus to Papeete to pay a visit to Customs to get the paperwork for duty free fuel. Next morning I went to the fuel dock and filled up with diesel before heading out through the reef at Passe Taapuna and setting a course for the north of Moorea. We had a fair wind for once so not to waste it I decided to forgo stopping at Moorea again and headed out for the Iles Sous le Vent. These comprise the western islands of the Society Islands, Huahine, Raiatea, Tahaa and Bora Bora.

We were making good progress with a nice beam wind until shortly after sunset when the wind died, progress was then fitful until in the end I started the engine and motored. With the dawn Huahine was in sight in the distance and although I had originally planned to miss this island out, I had a change of heart, a slight course alteration took me there.

Passing the reef to the west of the island was the sobering sight of a catamaran wrecked high and dry on the reef. I had heard about this whilst still in Tahiti, and had previously meet the American family briefly when I was in Shelter Bay Panama. They had sailed too close to the reef in the night and paid the price, fortunately they were all airlifted off safely.

A few miles further on I entered the reef by Passe Avapehi and anchored near by the town of Fare. Here in the anchorage was Jan and Richard on Morpheus, so it was good to see these friends again.

I spent a day with them on a motor car tour of the island, not something I normally do but it was interesting and we saw all the sights. Included amongst these were the sacred blue eyed eels in the river by the village of Faie.

On then for the 20 mile passage to the twin islands of Raiatea and Tahaa, both within the same encircling lagoon. I had a nice gentle beam wind of about 10 knots for this crossing. Entering by Passe Iriru between two motus I proceeded up to the head of Baie Faaroa to anchor. Here I took the dinghy up the navigable Aoppumau river, a good little trip. Opposite the site of the botanical gardens, closed for refurbishment, a man beckoned me across to the opposite bank and took me on a tour of his plantation. He gave me a green coconut to drink, very refreshing and showed me his bananas, taro, guava, squashes, cucumbers, mangos and more.

Truly paradise, I left with gifts of taro and bananas and some beautiful flowers. The people here are good.

Next day I motored inside the lagoon following the marked channel up to the North end of Raiatea and across to Tahaa where I followed the long Baie Haamene to anchor off the village at it's head.

It isn't always sunny in Polynesia and we had a day of rain and the cloud was down so I could barely see across the bay. I went ashore briefly in a period when it was just drizzle to get some bread from the supermarket but returning it rained and rained and getting back to the boat I had to strip off in the cockpit and ring out my shorts and vest before going below.

I went for a nice walk from Haamene bay over to the other, western side of the island to the village of Tiva, mainly on roads but very quiet ones, past vanilla plantations and also a track which turned out to be a dead end but with a very nice view down into the bay. It was good to get some exercise and see some more of the island.

That evening it blew up some and the wind was funnelling right down the bay making the anchorage very choppy and a lee-shore to boot. A disturbed night followed and I kind of regretted not moving anchorage yesterday instead of going for the long walk. With the wind at 25 knots it wasn't fun hauling the anchor and it came up covered in thick black mud, but there was no time to wash it off, it would have to wait. I moved around to Opu bay and picked up a mooring here. The wind still whistled over the low point but it was protected from the waves. The wind persisted next day and I would have stayed here but I was on a Pearl farm visitors mooring and they wanted it for their guests so I moved back to Riaitea and moored off Marina Apooiti. The one problem with French Polynesia is that most of the anchorages are deep, which with me having no windlass limited me somewhat at times. At least moored here I was conveniently close to Passe Rautoanui, the main all weather western pass through the reefs.

Early next morning with a better forecast I exited the reef and set a course for Bora Bora some 25 miles away. Apart from a brief period of calm I had a good sail. Richard and Jan in Morpheus past me later in their Island Packet 42. The southwest corner of the reef of Bora Bora is a long way offshore so needs a good offing, but helpfully is marked by a big beacon. Following the reef edge northwards I arrived at Passe Teavanui, the only entrance to the lagoon and was soon at the mooring field of the Bora Bora yacht club. Here Richard was helpfully by the only free mooring in his dinghy, they had seen me arrive through the pass chased by a big catamaran and kindly thought to save the mooring for me. The mooring was very close to the dock of the yacht club, I could almost step ashore for drinks. I moved to a mooring a little further out in the morning when one became free.

The forecast for the next week was not great with bad weather and high winds moving in and persisting all week so it was a period of hunkering down and waiting it out.

I did get to walk to Vaitape, the main town, a few times and I also dug out the Brompton from the forward stowage and got to cycle around the island, about 20 or so miles which was very enjoyable.

But it was time to leave French Polynesia, I had spent almost 4 months there. I suppose one question you could ask yourself about whether you like a place or not is whether you could live there. The answer is this case is yes. I liked the islands, the lagoons, the water, the climate, the people and the laid back lifestyle.

I started off the clearance process by visiting the gendarmerie and filling in all the forms, I just had to go back after the weekend and pick up my clearance for the Cook islands, about 600 miles away, where I am bound for next. The forecasts were looking improved for the next week so I was hoping for the best.

22. Passage to Tonga

"I tell you naught for your comfort,
Yea, naught for your desire,
Save that the sky grows darker yet
And the seas rise higher" (W.H Tilman)

I left Bora Bora on Monday, it was about midday when I got away after a delay with my clearance papers and a visit to the supermarket to spend my remaining Polynesian francs. In my muddle headed thoughts I was looking to arrive at Aitutaki before the weekend and catch the high tide on Friday about 11am thinking 485 miles should take 5 days so leave Monday arrive Friday. Wrong thats only 4 days travelling!

Wind and waves were a bit fiesty that first afternoon but the forecast was for the wind to lessen so ok and anyway it was not so fiesty as to prevent me cooking a proper meal that first evening (couscous, fried veg and sauce, since you ask!)

The wind did ease off in the night but don't you know it, down to about 8 to 10 knots so was I never going to make my 100 miles per day anyway. It stayed like that for 4 days, it was so easy to lose track of time and days, it was fairly calm conditions although since sailing almost directly downwind it was a little rolly at times.

One night I had a passenger aboard, just as it was getting dark a brown boobie was circling the boat determinedly and after one abortive effort landed on the solar panel, whereupon it began a thorough and vigorous preening session after which he settled down to roost with head tucked under wing. It stayed all night and left just after dawn next morning.

The light in the compass packed up but next morning I managed to solder in a new bulb. It was a little on the bright side and I thought would have to try and get a LED for it at some time rather than a normal bulb.

As you are not allowed to take any fruit or vegetables into the Cook islands with you, I had set off low on these and soon had only some onions left. At least I had lots of tinned stuff so wouldn't go hungry.

Before I reached Aitutaki we had a bit of a blow! The wind picked up Friday evening and blew strongly for 3 days. I got to about 6 miles off the entrance to the channel through the reef at Aitutaki about 6 am Sunday, but it was blowing about 25 knots, grey overcast sky, drizzling and threatening black cloud so I decided not to risk trying to get in. The entrance through the reef is long narrow and shallow and there is not much room once inside either. With no visibility I wasn't even going to look and be tempted so a simple decision really to carry on. Too many boats have been lost trying to enter harbours in poor conditions, I didn't want to make that mistake. A shame to miss out the Cook Islands but that's the way it was.

Soon the wind really picked up to about 30 knots and more in gusts, I handed the main and just ran under staysail, the sea was a bit boisterous.

Tuesday morning and there was still lots of wind, it hadn't really let up since Friday, I had never known it to be so windy for so long. The boat was still just running under staysail only which was pulling us along nicely. The weather had improved in that it had been sunny with some clouds but the constant movement of the boat made life a little hard.

What a great invention is tinned french casoulet though, you just have to heat it up and a complete meal is to be had, I was glad I had bought a few tins.

I judged that it was too windy to call in at Palmerston island as there is no sheltered anchorage there, just some exposed moorings perilously close to the reef. This was a great shame and if it continued it would be too unsafe to stop at Niue as there is no harbour there either, again just some moorings outside the reef. I was thinking that at least at Vava'u Tonga there is a well protected harbour with a straightforward entrance so if it continued like this it should be ok. Tonga was about 500 or so miles away so a ways to go.

Thursday night (I think it was) was particularly bad with the boat movement. My normal bunk was untenable, the other just as bad with the rolling and for a while I wedged myself in the quarter berth. Here I had to be scrunched up in the end to get wedged in so that wasn't so good either so I went back to the port berth with a lee-cloth up. Glad to say later the wind dropped a little and swell calmed down. I re-hoisted the main with 2 reefs and even got some yankee up.

I sighted Niue around 6pm Friday night, I was glad to see it before it went completely dark so I knew my course was ok and I wasn't going to run into it! It might have been possible to stop there as the weather was ok but I would have had a long night hove to off the island so I thought it best to carry on whilst I had better sailing weather. It was about 230 miles on to Vava'u Tonga from Niue.

Sunday morning I looked out of the hatch around 5 am and it was as black as the ace of spades, it seemed like the weather hadn't done with me yet. It came on to blow and rain, 35 knots or more, thoroughly unpleasant, I handed the main and was just under staysail again. After I got it sorted and checked my course I was going northeast rather than west as the wind had switched about 90 degrees from north to south so I got that put right then retired to the cabin dripping wet. It rained until the afternoon but stayed windy all day and night. The only saving grace was I had plenty of sea room, about 100 miles and there are no ships out here.

Hopefully I would get to Tonga for Monday, only since it was the other side of the international date line it would be Tuesday. I would lose a day and will be 1 day ahead of the UK. Fair does my head in even if I use the world clock on my iphone.

The area I was in is the South Pacific Convergence Zone, this is a notable zone and occurs where the southeast trades from transitory anticyclones to the south meet with the semipermanent easterly flow from the eastern South Pacific. It is noted for unstable weather with clouds, rain and thunderstorms. Captain John, a notable authority of the area nicknamed it the dangerous middle so sailing through this area is not to be taken lightly. Sometimes it can not be so bad but it seemed I had hit it at one of its bad times.

Approaching Toga I came around the north of the island and saw a humpback whale which was great, and then down the west side of the island to the channel in. I was glad that it was a fairly easy entrance although unmarked. I wasn't helped by it blowing really strong, a head wind of course once I got to the entrance. However I got far enough to pick up the lighted buoys before it was really dark, there was a full moon so should have been fine but it was very cloudy, I couldn't see the moon so it was no help.

I got in to Neiafu, Vavau around 8pm and picked up a mooring, pleased and relieved to be in safely after a tough passage of 14 days and 1275 nautical miles.

23. Kingdom of Tonga

"No man who has loved the sea can forsake her, ever." (Claud Worth)

A new country, the first job is to complete formalities. Arriving in the dark as I had, I had picked up a mooring buoy. Next morning I had to move over to the dockside flying a yellow quarantine flag. The first official to visit was the quarantine officer, to check that you are not bringing any banned products like fruit and vegetables in with you or carrying bugs on the boat. Then a trip into town, to the bank, work out the exchange rate and to get some local currency to pay the fees. Next to the customs office to fill in a great wadge of forms, always a trifle irksome because you have to repeat the same information ie boat name, your name, ships registration, length of boat etc etc over and over again on different forms. Lastly the health officer to see if you are healthy and not bringing disease with you. The fee for this goes to the local hospital. Then it was back to a mooring buoy.

The next few days were spent in Neiafu. I had a few jobs to do on the boat first. The major one was to overhaul the wind vane steering as a bush had gone on passage. To replace this I first had to take the self steering gear off the back of the boat so I could dissassemble it in the cockpit. Stripped down and cleaned up I replaced the bush and bearings, thankful that I had the spares on hand, reassembled and refitted. The last item was a bit tricky because it's a weighty beast and a dinghy not the most stable platform to work from.

There was some time for socialising, Dan on My Dream was here and Thom on Fathom and Rusty John and Oceana on Danika turned up a few days later. Neiafu is a small place and doesn't take much exploring but there is a good market for fruit and vegetables and the place comes alive on Saturdays when people gather and hang about in the streets. In between other jobs I took a walk over to the boatyard on the other side of the island for a look see and also went up Mount Talau. Well its stretching it a bit to call it a mountain, at 310m hardly a lofty eminence but it is the highest point in Vava'u and is a fine viewpoint to look out over the many islands and inlets that comprise the Vava'u group.

In French Polynesia it was chickens and roosters that were everywhere, here in Tonga it is pigs that roam about. Apart from the odd day the weather had not been great, with grey skies and lots of rain but when it improved it was time to head out to enjoy some of the other anchorages that are here. First stop was to anchor off the tiny island of Nuku, memorable for its fine white sandy spit at one end. On then to Vakaeitau Island, winding a way between small islands and reefs to cross the reef guarding the delightful bay where I anchored. Anchored here were Ken and Tracy who I had last seen in Portobelo, Panama, it was good to catch up over a bottle of wine in the cockpit.

There is just one family lives on the island, like all Togan islands heavily wooded. They held a Tongan feast for the cruisers anchored here, roast pig, chicken curry, raw fish marinated in coconut milk and a melange of different vegetable dishes. Two of the little girls dressed in the traditional bark cloth costumes did some Tongan dancing and there was a big fire burning under a huge banyan tree.

After some days I was out of bread, booze and fresh vegetables so I headed back to Neiafu to restock. I had a pleasant sail back the long way around as it were passing first north of Lape island and then south of Langito'o island, out towards Foeta island up past Luakmoko island past Kitu island and so back to Neiafu. Jan and Richard of Morpheus were here now so I joined them for happy hour at the bar.

Restocked with provisions, next day I dug out the bike and cycled down and across the causeway to Pangiamoto island and followed the roads first to

Hikakalea Beach then back tracking across to Utangake island until the road ran out overlooking Mala island. Although the islands are fairly low lying there were enough hills to make it hard work at times.

I had another bike ride on Vava'u to enable me to see more of the island, this up to Hila ki Tapana lookout to the north of the island, up a steep dirt track past plenty of Taro fields, it was hot hard work but worthwhile.

I decided to stay on in Neiafu for the Vava'u Blue Water Festival. Some of its attraction was that representatives from New Zealand Customs, Opua marina and Whangerai marina came over to give us cruisers the lowdown on New Zealand, which was very useful. They seem determined to try and make it as easy as possible for yachties to visit New Zealand and we seemed assured of a good welcome there. There are some restrictions on what you can take to New Zealand, for example no fruit or vegetables and no plants. They take their biosecurity seriously, they don't have fruit flies in New Zealand for instance. I had to say goodbye to my Aloe Vera plant that had been with me since the Canaries, which was a bit of a wrench, but I found a good home for it at the Aquarium cafe who were only too pleased to have it, they are valued plants here.

The festival kicked off with a sausage sizzle at the boatyard, who laid on free sausages and beer. For the official opening on the Monday we had a Tongan brass band playing for us - just like a colliery band back home although here the boys and men in the band all wear skirts called tupena and then an evening meal. On subsequent days there was a breakfast hosted by Whangarei marina, we visited a primary school where the children put on a show of dancing for us and a Tongan buffet was laid on by the parents, there was a barbecue and party at the Basque tavern, a humpback whale talk and pizza and finally a last night meal. As another cruiser pointed out the cost of the ticket for the festival was more than returned in terms of the meals we received.

Festival over, it was time to move on the the Ha'apai group about 70 miles south. I left early afternoon to be clear of the islands and reefs of the Vava'u group before dark and then an overnight passage to arrive just after first light. There are about 60 islands in this group only about 17 being inhabited, it is not much visited and has very little tourism. I skirted the first islands and anchored at Pangai the main settlement on the island of Lifuka. It is a sleepy little place, there is not much there and not much going on. It had been badly hit by cyclone Ian in 2014 which had caused much destruction. Half of the islands building had been destroyed and many of the rest had suffered serious damage. Three years later and some rebuilding was still underway.

It had been my intention to visit a few more of the islands and anchorages here but in the end I decided to give this a miss and head straight for Nuku'alofa on Tongatapu. All the pilot guides suggest you need someone to keep watch on the bow for reefs and I think I was feeling the strain of navigating through all the unmarked reefs a bit much on my own.

It was about 107 miles to Nuku'alofa so I left at midday and sailed westwards to clear the islands and reefs before turning south for another overnight passage. I had sort of company for this in the form of another yacht who followed me out and eventually overtook me, but I kept them in sight all night and through the next morning when I eventually lost sight of them in poor visibility and rain of a very grey and cloudy morning when the wind headed me. The entrance to Nuku'alofa is long and although wide, encumbered by shallows and reefs but with a distinct lack of markers to help you in. I didn't enjoy it. I was surprised to pass Dan in My Dream on his way out to New Zealand. I commented that it wasn't a nice day to be heading out as it was blowing about 20 knots, grey and rainy but he said he hoped it would get better.

I eventually got in and dropped anchor off the beach of Pangaimotu island. There were a few other boats here that I had seen from time to time on my travels across the Pacific.

Ashore is a beach bar - Big Momma's Yacht Club which offers a warm welcome. There is a little ferry to cross to Nuku'alofa itself which is the capital of Tonga so I went across for supplies and a look around. It is a bustling busy place with lots of shops, lots of stalls and quite a contrast to Neiafu. The palace of the King is here. Tonga always maintained its sovereignty and is the only Pacific nation to maintain its monarchical government.

The plan was to stop here a while until there was a suitable weather window to proceed to New Zealand. A lot of talk amongst the cruisers at Nuku'alofa is around a suitable weather window for the passage to New Zealand. It seems to be a passage that many are concerned about. I studied the weather and waited for the strong southerlies we were experiencing to pass before deciding on a departure date.

24. Passage to New Zealand

"Quite apart from the pleasures of sailing a boat, the sight and sound of the sea, the adventure of achieving some distant port aided only by the wind and ones own energy and skill, there are the unspiritually attractions of a life of comfort and security in a pleasant open air prison, with a minimum of shaving and washing, and without the trouble of undressing at night." (W.H Tilman)

Friday morning saw me taking the ferry across from Pangiamoto island to Nuka'alofa to get my clearance papers to leave. Harbours dues were paid in one office then to Customs for clearance. Shopping for a few provisions and then back to the boat on the ferry.

Provisioning for this trip is a little difficult as New Zealand restrictions are strict on what you can take in, for example no fruit or vegetables, dried pulses, popcorn etc etc so you need to stock up on just what you need but no more. This was tricky when the passage could take from 10 to 15 days depending on winds and weather.

Back at the boat I quickly readied for sailing and left by 2.30, just enough time to exit Tongapatu by the Elgia channel and be clear of all the reefs before sunset. The

Elgia channel has a distinct lack of markers of any kind so its eyeball pilotage assisted by electronic charts on the ipad. The electronic charts have to be treated with caution as along with most of the Pacific islands they can be as much as 300 metres out in position.

It was just then a question of settling down to the routine of a long passage. For the first days the winds were light with some calms so progress was slow and my first noon to noon run a disappointing 71 miles, but gradually we got better winds in both strength and direction. I had a bit of disaster on the night of the 5th day. I had been running under light winds of about 8 knots with a poled out yankee and main. At sunset despite the light winds as a precaution as I normally do I had put a reef in the main and taken a few rolls in the yankee. Just before midnight as I was taking a short nap I awoke with the boat heeled well over, the wind shrieking and torrential rain. It was a wild and stormy night. Turning out I rolled away the yankee with a struggle and reefed the main down to the third reef, by the time I was done I was soaked through.

Next morning I discovered that the yankee had ripped which was a blow but I could swop it out for the working jib that I carried and in the event that was a good choice of sail for the wind for the rest of the passage.

On the 8th day, a lovely sunny day with a good wind and pretty flat seas, I spotted a sail astern and it turned out to be my friends Jan and Richard on Morpheus so we were able to chat on the vhf for a while before they overtook me. My daily runs were improving, 99 miles, 107 miles, 134 miles and now I was about 70 miles from the Bay of Islands. By sunset I was doing over 5 knots and just 43 miles off so I slowed the boat down by reefing the main more and finally dropping the staysail as I didn't want to arrive in the dark. By dawn I was 10 miles off and although I could see the flash of the lighthouse on Cape Brett, the coast was coyly hidden in cloud and murk. The weather though gradually cleared and the coast revealed as I entered the Bay of Islands and made my way into Opua. There were lots of boats about. Midmorning saw me alongside the customs pontoon to await customs clearance and quarantine. No problem with this as I had notified them of my imminent arrival by email before leaving Tonga and a VHF call once in NZ waters as the regulations require. Then onto a berth in the marina. A bit tricky this with a wind astern and some tide too but berthing was successfully accomplished without hitting anything.

Great I had done it - an 11 day passage of 1034 n miles which means I had sailed 7478 miles across the Pacific to arrive in New Zealand.

I had sailed 15,400 miles since leaving the UK and half way around the world. A beer or two was in order that night.

Appendix 1

The Boat

Sea Bear is a Vancouver 28, it was designed by Robert Harris and Sea Bear was built by Northshore in 1987.

She is of fibreglass construction with an encapsulated keel. She is 28 feet (8.54 m) overall in length with a beam of 8ft 8inches (2.64 m). She is cutter rigged which means she generally carries three sails. A mainsail and two foresails, that is a yankee and a staysail.

She is tiller steered and is fitted with a windvane self steering system.

Underneath the cockpit seats are 3 lockers, one holds the life-raft the other two, things like the outboard for the tender, fenders, mooring warps, a spare anchor, buckets, brushes, a boat hook, a hosepipe.

Instrument displays for the depth, speed, log and windspeed are mounted on a panel above the hatch entrance to the cabin. The hatch leads to the companionway steps leading down into the cabin.

Below decks starting from the aft. To the port side there is "wet" locker for hanging water proofs, a locker which holds the fuel tank for the cooker, which is of the old fashioned pressurised paraffin type with two burners and an oven. Forward of this is the galley sink which is supplied by two foot pumps, one supplies seawater, the other fresh water from the water tanks which are under the cabin sole (floor). Above the sink and stove are lockers which hold crockery and some food supplies. To starboard there is a quarter berth which is mainly tucked away under the cockpit. The end of this berth provides a seat for the chart table and under is a locker which I use for food supplies. Under the chart table is a drawer for storing paper charts and also a locker where I store most of my tools. Ranged on this side are a shelf which are used for log and pilot books, the electrical switch panel for lights and the instruments such as the vhf radio, GPS and AIS.

Forward are two saloon berths, one to each side of a centre mounted table with folding flaps. Under each berth are lockers which hold various stores and spares. Above the berths are more lockers and two bookshelves.

Forward again to port there is a hanging wardrobe with on the starboard side a sink. Forward again are the heads and forward of this a storage area mainly used for sail stowage but also roomy enough for a folding bicycle.

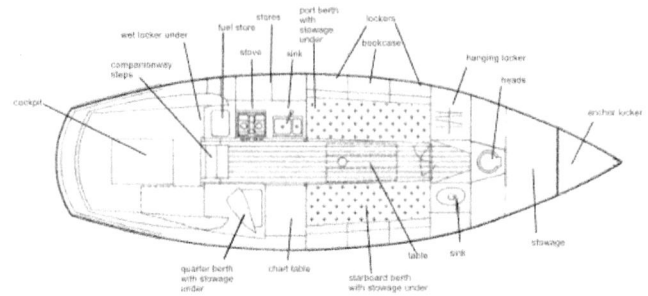

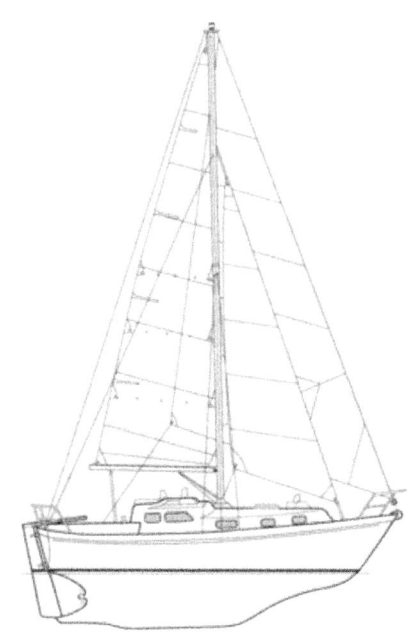

Appendix 2
Glossary

Aback - Normally a sail is sheeted in on the opposite side from which the wind comes. A sheet is the rope attached to the rear lower corner of a sail and used to control it. A sail is said to be aback when the sheet and the wind are on the same side.

AIS - automatic identification system, a piece of electronic gadgetry which broadcasts and receives a signal from a ship giving its position, speed and heading and sometimes more.

Beating - sailing with the wind forward of the beam, said to be beating to windward.

Cardinal mark - a special type of buoy used to mark something of danger.

Cruising Shute - a large sail of light material used in lighter wind conditions.

Cutter - when a yacht has 2 foresails , one behind the other it is said to be cutter rigged.

Genoa - a large foresail.

GPS - global positioning system.

Gunwale - edges of a boats side above the level of the deck.

Gybe - when the boom and the mainsail passes from one side of the boat to the other. Can be either a deliberate manoeuvre or accidental - an accidental one is to be avoided as it can cause damage.

Hove to - with the jib aback and the tiller lashed, the opposing forces of wind in the sails and the tiller trying to turn the boat an equilibrium is reached where the boat lies.

Lee cloth - a canvas cloth that is rigged alongside a berth and stop one sliding or rolling off the berth with the boats movement.

Log - as in log book, a book where you keep records of time distance position weather and any incidents or remarks etc.

Log - as in an instrument that measures speed and distance travelled through the water.

Lying ahull - Taking all sails down and letting the boat lie as it will to the waves. One technique sometimes used in gale or storm conditions.

Main - short for Main sail.

Reaching - a point of sailing where the wind is from the beam or side of the boat. Generally the fastest and most comfortable point of sailing.

Reefing - the process of reducing the size of a sail to make it more manageable as the wind increases in strength. Generally there are 3 fixed reef positions so we speak of 1st, 2nd and 3rd reefs.

Reef - also rocks or coral patch partially or wholly submerged and posing a danger to a boat.

Sextant - instrument used to measure the angle between the sun or other planetary body and the horizon and used to calculate ones position on the earth.

Snuffer - a sort of a sock that can be pulled down over a sail to make handling it easier when taking it down or handing it.

Sprayhood - a framed canvas hood that provides protection from weather and spray.

Spreaders - horizontal arms from the mast which provide bracing and direction for the standing rigging.

Spring line - a type of mooring line, mooring lines have different names depending on where they are attached to.

Standing rigging - the wires which hold the mast upright.

Staysail - a foresail which goes aft of the Jib, Genoa or Yankee

Swinging mooring - A mooring that a boat ties up to via its bow and can swing according to the tide and wind.

Washboards - boards that fit in the hatchway to shut it off.

Yankee - a foresail with a high cut foot.

Printed in Great Britain
by Amazon